Harbor Lights *of* Home

By

Edgar A. Guest

Verse—

> The Light of Faith
> A Heap o' Livin'
> Just Folks
> Poems of Patriotism
> The Path to Home
> When Day Is Done
> The Passing Throng
> Rhymes of Childhood
> Harbor Lights of Home

Illustrated—

> All That Matters

Prose—

> What My Religion Means to Me
> Making the House a Home
> My Job as a Father
> You Can't Live Your Own Life

Gift Books—

> Mother
> Home
> Friends
> You

Harbor Lights of Home

By

Edgar A. Guest

The Reilly & Lee Co.

Chicago

Harbor Lights of Home

Dedicated

To the best friends, the best neighbors,
the best citizens in the world—the home folks!

Harbor Lights of Home

A minister hath given you
The name you'll wear for aye.
I wish he could have shriven you
And washed your faults away.

E. A. G.

The Story of the Title

In May, 1928, Mr. Guest's publishers offered a prize of $1,000 for the best title for his Ninth Book of Verse. From nearly half a million suggested titles the three judges unanimously chose the title submitted by the Reverend M. S. Rice. The prize winner was invited to tell the story of how he came to make his choice. Dr. Rice responded as follows:

When it was suggested that the interested public should name the next book of my dear friend Edgar A. Guest, the title, *Harbor Lights of Home,* came to my mind as by an intuition. I am not accustomed to competitive suggestions, but the aptness of the name seemed to me so clear I could not resist offering it.

I know Mr. Guest; I know his home; I know how beautifully his pen is constantly finding the genuine truths of a genuine home for the guidance of all other homes.

These are difficult days in our social world. Many things are drifting and uncertain. The home is imperiled. It is the primary foundation of all our social relationship. He who strikes at the home will shake the fundamentals of all government. There seem to be many forces which are working that way.

Edgar A. Guest is in my judgment the finest force in America to-day, in defense of the home. With homely, and beautiful, and heart-touching phrases and stories, he is setting clearly before our country the fact of parental love and affection, and making clear the way for our socially troubled day, out of its storm and threatening darkness, into the secure harbor of a real home life.

One night, with my boys, I found myself in our little boat along a strange shore of a great lake, and no harbor was to be had. We were inexperienced sailors, and our chart did not show a course to the nearest safety. I drew a line across the chart from where we were to a lighthouse fifty miles away and, setting my compass on the line, figured as best I could the reading we should sail. For three hours we sailed straight into the darkness. No one can ever describe for me the feeling I had when out of that gloom before us came the flash of the light we sought.

Edgar Guest is setting, in an unfailing gleam before our generation, the genuine guidance of the Harbor Lights of Home. I shall most surely hope this latest volume of his may send its beckoning cheer across an even larger horizon than any of its predecessors, and that it may everywhere be as welcome as was the gleam of that lighthouse that dark night to me.

M. S. RICE.

Detroit, June, 1928.

INDEX

Poem	Page
Age	22
At Pinehurst	157
At the Journey's End	175
Aunt Jane Worried	92
Bad Golfer Who Was Good, The	65
Battered Dream Ship, The	109
Beneath the Stars	112
Best Land, The	33
Bird Nests	149
Bombing Squad Flies Over, A	182
Bride and Groom	85
Candy-Man, The	107
Canterbury Bells	150
Checking the Day	79
Children Know, The	185
City Home, The	181
Common Dog, The	161
Contentment	21
Counting the Babies	141
Cynic, The	127
Dead Oak Tree, The	32
Death, the Collector	125
Dreams	97
Dub Golfer, The	116
Enriched	50
Equipment	91
Fate Talks About Men	87
Father Gives His Version	29
Few New Teeth, A	83
Fine Arts, The	121

Index

Poem	Page
First Easter, The	71
First Watch, The	47
Fisherman's Luck	86
Flag, The	137
Fool, The	131
For Fish and Birds	74
Friend, A	134
Future, The	143
Gardeners	119
Gentle Man, The	93
Giant Stories	99
Grace	96
Grandpa's Walking Stick	17
Had Youth Been Willing to Listen	106
Hard Job, The	101
Her Awful Brother	129
Hint, A	115
His Philosophy	63
Home, The	173
Home Town, The	111
Honest People	70
Horn Honker, The	133
"I Didn't Think and I Forgot"	98
If To Be Clever	95
I Go Back Twenty Years	25
I Make An Experiment	177
Individuality	117
Inn-Keeper Makes Excuses, The	23
In the Garden	18
Intimate Tale, An	153
In Time of Trial	147
Journey, The	26
Joy of Getting Home, The	57
Keys to the Car, The	39
Kidnaped by a Dream	155

Index

Poem	Page
Life on the Earth	164
Life's Needs	102
Lights of Home, The	15
Like Calls to Like	37
Marbles and Money	43
Memorial Day	176
Men of Science	144
Merit and the Throng	77
Mind, The	67
Missing Man, The	73
Modern Barber, The	41
Modern Clothesline, The	179
Mother Finds Rest, A	145
Mother Tells Her Story, The	27
My Aunt's Bonnet	55
My Life	75
New Car, The	64
Night	163
No Honey-Gatherer	89
Old Hat, The	49
Old Prospector Talks, The	44
Old Sailor Talks, The	90
On Church Building	82
Organist, The	124
Our House	69
Perils of a Public Speaker	113
Pixley Folks	19
Plea, A	53
Possession	122
Prayer, A	31
Prayer for a Little Girl	140
Question of Sight, A	158

Index

Poem	Page
Said the Carpenter to Me	61
Salesman Gets a Shock, The	36
Sea-Dreams	103
Sentiment	54
She Wouldn't Go to Bed	59
Singing Bird, The	132
Study the Rules	108
Style	118
Success	180
Summer	126
Summer Day, A	58
Team Work	105
Then and Now	167
Theory and Practice	170
Time	165
To a Little Girl	151
To the June Bride	171
Tragedies of Innocence, The	104
Twilight	169
Two Worlds	81
Unchanged	160
Up and Down the Lanes of Love	45
Waster, The	78
What a Man Likes	35
Who Builds a House	148
Who Gets the Watch and Chain	128
Wild Flowers, The	174
Wise, The	123
Worst of Pests, The	183
Young Doctor, The	135
Younger Generation, The	139
Youth and the World	51

The Lights of Home

Much I've done and much I've seen,
To many places I have been,
But to me there's no delight
Like the lights of home at night.
Porch globe twinkling 'from afar,
Window lights which softer are,
Shining through the inky gloom
From a peaceful, happy room.

I've seen lights on ships at sea,
Lights that flash incessantly,
Beacon lamps, and those that shine
In some merchant's costly sign,
But my pulses faster beat
As I turn a little street
And I see the lights of home
Twinkling at me through the gloam.

Rest is here, they seem to say,
Peace is here to close the day,
Love is waiting to embrace
You within this little place,

Hurry faster! Hurry in!
Where there's neither hate nor sin
Nor the cruelty and care
Of the greedy world out there.

Hurry in and sit you down,
And forget the noisy town.
Shut the door and put away
All the burdens of the day.
Come, let loved ones stroke your cheek,
Let them laugh to hear you speak,
Here all selfish bickerings cease,
Here are love and rest and peace.

GRANDPA'S WALKING STICK

My grandpa once was very sick
And now he's got a walking stick,
Coz one of his legs, as he says to me,
Isn't quite so good as it used to be;
And he can't run and he daresen't kick
Coz he'd fall if he hadn't his walking stick.

When my grandpa comes to our house to stay
I like to carry his stick away,
And put it in places where he can't see,
Then he can't get up to come after me.
And he shouts out loud: "Hey! Everyone!
Who knows where my other leg has gone?

"I had it here by my chair and now
It's disappeared from its place somehow.
I'll bet this little Miss Mischief here
Knows something about it, she looks so queer.
Was it you, who carried my leg away?"
"Maybe 'twas eat by a bear," I say.

Then he can't get up and he can't move round
Till I come and tell him his leg is found.
The bear didn't swallow it after all,
He must have got frightened and let it fall.
Then my grandpa laughs till his sides are sore,
And we hippety-hop to the candy store.

IN THE GARDEN

I sometimes get weary of people, and weary of
      being polite;
I sometimes grow tired of the dull man, and some-
      times am bored by the bright.
And then when my nerves are a-tingle I walk in
      the yard that is ours,
And I thank the good Lord for the comfort of
      songsbirds and blue skies and flowers.

I never grow tired of the martens which circle about
      overhead;
I never grow weary of robins—there is nothing
      about them I dread.
I smile when I see them returning, I sigh when at
      last they depart,
And perhaps it's because they are never vindictive,
      or petty, or smart.

And the trees don't expect to be talked to. I can lie
      there and dream in the shade,
And not have to think up an answer to some dreary
      question that's made.
So I often slip into my garden when I'm weary of
      hearing things said,
And thank the good Lord for my roses and trees
      and the birds overhead.

PIXLEY FOLKS

Sometimes I git to thinkin' o' the days o' youth, an'
    then
There comes a-troopin' through my mind th' wimmin
    folk an' men
I used ter know in Pixley, an' I sit with 'em awhile,
A-livin' all th' fun we knew before we put on style:
A-dancin' all th' dances, th' lancers an' q'drilles,
A-goin' to th' huskin' bees an' picnics on th' hills;
An' I quite ferget I'm livin' on a crowded city street,
Where I don't know a quarter of th' people that I
    meet.

I settle in my arm chair, an' I light my meerschaum
    pipe,
An' then I'm back in Pixley with the apples red an'
    ripe.
I'm makin' eyes at Agnes, which is wrong I must
    allow,
Coz she was married long ago an' has four babies
    now.
An' I'm pokin' fun at Lydy, who was in for any
    joke,
But she has married wealthy—still out yonder in th'
    smoke
She is still the laughin' lassie, free from all the
    haughty airs
That wimmin folk think needful when they marry
    millionaires.

Then I steal a kiss from Nellie, an' I hear her say
    "No, no!"
Th' way she did a thousand times, but never meant
    it, though.
An' again from church we're comin', and th' hour is
    gettin' late
An' we stand awhile a-gabbin', she a-swingin' on th'
    gate,
A-tellin' of her uncles an' her aunts, an' how they
    were,
While all that I was wantin' was to stay an' talk of
    her.
An' again I'm gettin' ready jes' to ask her to be
    mine,
An' again she ups an' leaves me, sayin' "Ed, it's after
    nine."
O, I tell you what! It's funny, when I think about
    it all,
An' I kinder get to broodin' an' th' old days I recall
When there warn't no automobiles, warn't no prob-
    lem plays an' such,
When th' only fault with young folks was they loved
    t' play too much;
When there warn't no style about us, one warn't
    richer than another,
When we didn't think of money, never snubbed a
    poorer brother;
An' to see 'em now with riches, an' ashamed to even
    say
That they ever lived in Pixley—Why, *my soul* is
    there to-day! 20

CONTENTMENT

Money and fame and health alone
Are not enough for a man to own;
For healthy men are heard to sigh
And men of wealth go frowning by,
And one with fame may play his part
With a troubled mind and a heavy heart.
If these three treasures no joy possess,
How shall a man find happiness?

Health comes first in the famous three,
But cripples can smile, as we all must see;
Fame is sweet, as we all must own,
But the happiest hearts are not widely known.
Money is good, when it's truly earned,
But peace with fortune is not concerned,
For the bravest and loveliest souls we know
Have little of silver and gold to show.

Yet there must be a way to the goal we seek,
A path to peace for the strong and weak,
And it must be open for all to fare,
In spite of life's sorrows and days of care.
For those who have suffered the most the while
Look out on the world with the tenderest smile,
And those who have little of wealth to boast
Are often the ones that we love the most.

So I fancy the joy which men strive to win
Is born of something which lies within,
A strain of courage no care can break,
A love for beauty no thief can take—
For they are the happiest souls of earth
Who gather the treasures of gentle worth—
The pride of neighbors, the faith of friends
And a mind at peace when the sun descends.

AGE

How strange is age, that season of decay
. Which all men dread yet strongly hope to gain,
    And all men wish their loved ones to attain.
We pity those whose strength has slipped away.
The tired old people, done with work and play,
    Once more as children, keep the window pane
    And watch the world's swift moving human train
Bearing the freightage of the busy day.

Not to grow old, in youth a man must die.
    The price of age is fading sound and sight
And wrinkled foreheads and the sitting by
    While younger hearts press forward in the fight.
We know that age puts out ambition's fire,
Yet to grow old is every man's desire.

THE INN-KEEPER MAKES EXCUSES

"Oh, if only I had known!"
    Said the keeper of the inn.
"But no hint to me was shown,
    And I didn't let them in.

"Yes, a star gleamed overhead,
    But I couldn't read the skies,
And I'd given every bed
    To the very rich and wise.

"And she was so poorly clad,
    And he hadn't much to say!
But no room for them I had,
    So I ordered them away.

"She seemed tired, and it was late
    And they begged so hard, that I
Feeling sorry for her state,
    In the stable let them lie.

"Had I turned some rich man out
    Just to make a place for them,
'Twould have killed, beyond a doubt,
    All my trade at Bethlehem.

"Then there came the wise men three
　　To the stable, with the morn,
Who announced they'd come to see
　　The great King who had been born.

"And they brought Him gifts of myrrh,
　　Costly frankincense and gold,
And a great light shone on her
　　In the stable, bleak and cold.

"All my patrons now are dead
　　And forgotten, but to-day
All the world to peace is led
　　By the ones I sent away.

"It was my unlucky fate
　　To be born that Inn to own,
Against Christ I shut my gate—
　　Oh, if only I had known!"

I GO BACK TWENTY YEARS

I'm just an old fool, twenty years we've been wed,
And the craziest notion came into my head,
I remembered the way I'd made love to her then,
And I thought to myself I'll just try it again.
I'll court her once more in my old foolish way,
Just to see how she'll act and to hear what she'll say.

So I bought her some roses, a few in a box,
Just by way of commencing my series of shocks,
And all through the supper I looked at her so,
With that sad pensive look which all young lovers
    know,
And I patted her hand and kept calling her "dear,"
And she said to the children: "Your father is queer!"

I kissed her and rumpled her silver-tinged hair,
Rubbed my beard on her cheek, and she seemed not
    to care.
I said: "You are lovely! This wide world around
I am sure that your equal could never be found."
I praised the long lash on her eye's lovely lid,
Thinking she wouldn't like all that gush—but she
    did!

THE JOURNEY

From birth to death the pathway leads
   'Neath changing skies of blue and gray.
   How far the journey none can say,
At Heaven's gate meet all the creeds.

For some the road is long and straight.
   For some the way is rough and steep.
   But all must work and all must weep
And all must come to Heaven's gate.

Then why for words should friends divide?
   And why should comrades change to foes,
   Disputing what no mortal knows?
Why make of forms the things of pride?

The same port waits the great and low.
   For all the journey is the same,
   And who shall say that praise or blame
Shall come from what we couldn't know?

He wisest lives who trusts the plan
   By which he treads the ways of earth,
   Who gives himself to deeds of worth
And brothers with his fellow man.

THE MOTHER TELLS HER STORY

When first I met your father, it was at a wedding,
    dears,
And he wore a high white collar which stretched
    up to his ears,
He was thin and short and nervous, and his dress
    suit didn't fit,
And I didn't like the way he dressed his hair a little
    bit.
It was parted in the middle and it lopped across his
    brow—
And I never dreamed that evening I'd be married
    to him now.

I knew a dozen fellows who were handsomer than
    he,
And all of them were richer, and they thought a
    lot of me;
They brought me flowers and candy each time they
    came to call—
So this meeting with your father didn't mean much
    after all.
And besides his ways annoyed me—I'd have told
    him if I dared
That I didn't like his manner and the *vulgar way
    he stared.*

Well, next Sunday after dinner he came up to call
on me

And stayed so long that Grandma then invited him
for tea.

After that he came so often that your Grandpa used
to say:

"That skinny gawk is driving all the healthy stock
away!"

But somehow I'd grown to like him, and I marveled
that I could,

For he never tried to kiss me—though I often wished
he would.

Now that's all there is to tell you—by next June I
was his bride,

But before that I had made him part his hair upon
the side,

And I'd made him change his collars, and I'd slicked
him up a lot—

For I taught him what he should do, and the things
which he should not.

But don't tell him that I've told you. That's the way I
met your dad.

Would I do the same thing over? Well, he hasn't
been so bad!

FATHER GIVES HIS VERSION

Well, you see, I met your mother at a wedding, long
      ago,
And though I was four-and-twenty, up to then I
      didn't know
That in all our busy city, which I'd traveled up and
      down,
There was such a lovely creature, with such lustrous
      eyes of brown.
But the minute that I saw her I just stared and
      stared and stared,
And right then I would have hugged her and kissed
      her—if I'd dared!

She was acting as the bridesmaid, I was best man
      for the groom,
And of course the bride was lovely, but the loveliest
      in the room
Wasn't just then getting married—'twas my thought
      as I stood there—
For I couldn't keep from staring at your mother, I
      declare,
And I couldn't keep from thinking, as we knelt there,
      side by side,
There must be another wedding, and then she must
      be my bride.

Well, the wedding party scattered, bride and groom
      and guests and all,
But I asked that lovely bridesmaid if she'd let me
      come to call.
Well, she blushed and gave permission, and when
      Sunday evening came
I bought a box of candy, with a very famous name,
And I went up there to see her, and her Pa and Ma
      were there,
And I wanted *so* to kiss her—but of course I didn't
      dare.

Now that's how I met your mother—and 'twas
      twenty years ago,
And there was another wedding—just the one I'd
      longed to know,
For one lovely Sunday evening, when I went up
      there to call,
I caught her up and kissed her, as we lingered in
      the hall,
And we planned right then to marry—it was love
      that made me bold—
Now that's how I met your mother—but don't tell
      her that I told.

A PRAYER

Grant me, O Lord, this day to see
The need this world may have for me;
      To play the friend
      Unto the end;
To bear my burden and to keep
My courage, though the way be steep.

Grant me, O Lord, to set aside
The petty things of selfish pride;
      To toil without
      Too much of doubt;
To meet what comes of good or ill
And be a gracious neighbor, still.

Grant me, O Lord, to face the rain
And not too bitterly complain;
      Nor let a joy
      My calm destroy;
But teach me so to live that I
Can brother with each passer-by.

THE DEAD OAK TREE

An oak tree died the other day
  Despite my constant care;
Now men must carry it away
  And leave my garden bare.

It came to leaf in early spring.
  To live 'twas guaranteed;
Man is so vain and proud a thing,
  He vaunted God, indeed.

For how can mortal guarantee
  The breath of life, and say
That he can keep within a tree
  What God may take away?

It cannot be that man can sense,
  As do the sun and rain,
What living trees experience
  Of loneliness and pain.

I think they never heard it sigh,
  Nor ever dreamed a tree
Could, broken-hearted, pine and die,
  Who wrote that guarantee.

THE BEST LAND

If I knew a better land on this glorious world of
    ours,
Where a man gets bigger money and is working
    shorter hours;
If the Briton or the Frenchman had an easier life
    than mine,
I'd pack my goods this minute and I'd sail across
    the brine.
But I notice when an alien wants a land of hope
    and cheer,
And a future for his children, he comes out and
    settles here.

Here's the glorious land of Freedom. Here's the
    milk and honey goal
For the peasant out of Russia, for the long sub-
    jected Pole.
It is here the sons of Italy and men of Austria turn
For the comfort of their bodies and the money they
    can earn.
And with all that men complain of, and all that
    goes amiss,
There's no happier, better nation on the world's
    broad face than this.

So I'm thinking when I listen to the wails of dis
    content,
And some foreign disbeliever spreads his evil senti
    ment,
That the breed of hate and envy that is sowing
    sin and shame
In this glorious land of Freedom should go back
    from whence it came.
And I hold it is the duty, rich or poor, of every
    man
Who enjoys this country's bounty, to be ALL
    American.

WHAT A MAN LIKES

This is what a man likes: a blue sky and a stream,
The lily pads off yonder and the shore with gold
    agleam,
The west wind gently blowing for then the fishing's
    sure—
A friend to share the glory and a bass to take the
    lure.

This is what a man likes: a day away from things,
A day where dreams are golden and malice never
    stings,
A friend to read his heart to, who'll keep the tale
    secure,
A reel that's running freely and a bass to take the
    lure.

This is what a man likes: a chance to test his skill,
The hazard of disaster and a struggle's surging
    thrill,
The joy of honest hunger and hardships to endure,
The gulls to fly above him and a bass to take the
    lure.

This is what a man likes: a friend to share his boat,
The freedom of the open, an old and shabby coat.
For all the aches of failure, 'tis here he finds a
    cure—
A haunt God made for fishing, and a bass to take the
    lure.

THE SALESMAN GETS A SHOCK

The salesman saw his shabby clothes, and eyed him
    head to toe;
So rough a looking man, thought he, could not be
    good to know;
And since he sold expensive cars, which only rich
    men buy,
To sell the ragged-looking man he did not even try.

The stranger walked among the cars and looked the
    models o'er,
The youthful salesman passed him by a dozen times
    or more;
Not once he paused to talk to him, he scorned the
    proffered smile,
And looked about for richer men who might be more
    worth while.

The manager came out at last and saw the shabby
    man.
His hand went out in welcome as he shouted: "Hello,
    Dan!"
"Hello, Bill," said the shabby man, "my daughter
    wants a car
And I've been noseying around to see how good they
    are!

"Send up the red one over there, she likes to cut a
    dash,"
And reaching in his wallet he drew out the price in
    cash.

"My women wear the style for me. You know my
    ways are quaint.
By gosh," said he, "I think that boy has fallen in a
    faint!"

They brought the youthful salesman to, and sent
    him home to rest.
"Don't ever judge a man," said they, "by how he
    may be dressed.
You lost a good cash customer, but write this lesson
    down:
'Not all the worthwhile people strut in broadcloth
    'round the town.'"

LIKE CALLS TO LIKE

If you walk as a friend you will find a friend
    wherever you choose to fare,
If you go with mirth to a far strange land you will
    find that mirth is there.
For the strangest part of this queer old world is
    that like will join with like,
And who walks with love for his fellowmen an
    answering love will strike.

Here each of us builds his little world, and chooses
    its people, too;
Though millions trample the face of earth, each
    life touches but the few.
And the joy you'll find as you venture forth your
    fortune or fame to make,
Lies not in some stranger's power to say, for it's
    all in the joy you take.

If you walk in honor then honest men will meet
    you along the way,
But if you be false you will find men false, wher-
    ever you chance to stray.
For good breeds good and the bad breeds bad; we
    are met by the traits we show.
Love will find a friend at the stranger's door where
    hate would find a foe.

For each of us builds the world he knows, which
    only himself can spoil,
And an hour of hate or an hour of shame can ruin
    a life of toil.
And though to the farthermost ends of earth your
    duty may bid you fare
If you walk with truth in your heart as a friend,
    you will find friends waiting there.

THE KEYS TO THE CAR

The keys to the car! Oh, the keys to the car,
What a terrible, horrible burden they are!
  Whenever we travel
  The concrete or gravel,
Or visit the neighbors or go as we please,
  I start in to fumble
  And foolishly mumble
This query: "Oh, what did I do with the keys?"

I go through my pockets like mad on the quest,
I go through my trousers, my coat and my vest—
  I've keys for the clock
  And the doors that I lock,
I've keys I possess and don't know what they are,
  I've keys for the closet,
  The safety deposit—
But what did I do with the keys to the car?

I've gloves and I've papers, I've letters and bills
And all of the stuff that a man's pockets fills,
  I've matches, a token,
  A knife that is broken,

The mangled remains of a ruined cigar,
   I've loose paper-clippers
   And finger-nail snippers—
But where, yes, oh where, are the keys to the car?

Nell asks: "Are you sure?" and I answer her:
      "Madam,
Never mind your suggestions, I tell you I had 'em!
   Just look on me pleasantly,
   I'll find 'em presently,
They're somewhere about me and cannot be far;
   They're here, that's conclusive,
   Not lost—just elusive,
Just wait till I find 'em—those keys to the car."

THE MODERN BARBER

The old-time barber used to be a genial sort of
    cuss;
He gathered up the gossip and he'd give it all to us.
His language wasn't polished, and some epithets he'd
    use
To strengthen his opinions or to decorate the news.
He'd snip and talk, and talk and snip, and now and
    then he'd let
Us see the ladies' pictures in the old Police Gazette.

The old-time barber didn't need an education vast,
'Twas enough to know the fighters of the present
    and the past.
And in the baseball season he could get along right
    well
With the home team's printed schedule and a yarn
    or two to tell.
Then, as we waited for our turn, we never had to
    fret,
We could look at all the ladies in the old Police
    Gazette.

But now the old-time barber and his shop have
    passed away;
Men no longer talk with freedom when they visit
    him to-day.

For the women folk are sitting round the room in
      every chair,
And the modern barber's busy bobbing many a
      matron's hair.
Now it's "Vogue" and the "Pictorial" his waiting
      patrons get,
Instead of that old favorite, the pink Police Gazette!

The modern barber's had to learn a line of talk
      that's new;
The language of the prize ring and the diamond
      will not do.
Now he snips and chats of fashions, weddings, din-
      ner parties, teas;
And tells 'em who's been in to get their tresses
      bobbed for these.
There is never talk of prize fight or a horse race
      or a bet,
For his shop is now a parlor, where there is no
      Police Gazette.

MARBLES AND MONEY

Ed and John were little boys in the long ago,
Playing marbles day by day, just like boys you know.
Ed was clever, so was John. Ed one difference
    bore—
Winning marbles when he played made him wish
    for more.
Heavier grew his little sack, still on winning bent—
Ed had more than he could use, but was not content.

John played marbles now and then, never lost them
    all;
Had enough to join the game when the boys would
    call,
Played at baseball, climbed the trees, loved the birds,
    and knew
Many a thrill of doing things Ed would never do.
Kept his marbles in a sack smaller far than Ed's;
Hadn't more than fifty mibs, blues and whites and
    reds.

"John," said Ed one day to him, still on marbles
    bent,
"I've a thousand in my sacks, but I'm not content.
Just how many now have you?" Answered John,
    "A few.
Fifty marbles, I should say, but I've more than
    you."

"More than I?" said Ed, surprised, "surely that
     can't be!"
"Yes," said John, "I've more than you—I've all I
     want, you see."

Rich man, piling wealth on wealth, catch John's
     point of view!
Who has all he wants to-day is richer far than you.

THE OLD PROSPECTOR TALKS

Gold is found in the hills, and then
Carried back to the haunts of men.
And two of us came in the early days
To pan the streams for the dirt that pays.

And we stuck it out for a time, till he
Got sick of the game which enchanted me.
And he went back to the town one day
To get his gold in an easier way.

He quit these hills and he left me cold
To scramble with men for his bit of gold.
Now some like walls and roofs and rooms,
But I like mountains where thunder booms,

And skies and trees and the open plains
Where a man must work for the bit he gains.

So I've stayed right here and I've dreamed my dreams
And smoked my pipe by these running streams,

And kept my cabin up here alone,
With all this beauty to call my own.
I've taken my gold with pick and pan
And sent it back to be stained by man.

I've wrestled with rocks and streams for mine
And made my friendships with fir and pine.
Now the world down there may think me odd,
But maybe I won't seem queer to God.

UP AND DOWN THE LANES OF LOVE

Up and down the lanes of love,
With the bright blue skies above,
And the grass beneath our feet,
Oh, so green and Oh, so sweet!
There we wandered, boy and girl,
Sun-kissed was each golden curl;
Hand in hand we used to stray,
Hide-and-seek we used to play;
Just a pair of kids were we,
Laughing, loving, trouble free.

Up and down the lanes of love
With the same blue skies above,

Next we wandered, bride and groom,
With the roses all in bloom;
Arm in arm we strolled along,
Life was then a merry song,
Laughing, dancing as we went,
Lovers, cheerful and content;
No one else, we thought, could be
Quite so happy as were we.

Up and down the lanes of love,
Dark and gray the skies above;
Hushed the song-birds' merry tune,
Withered every rose of June.
Grief was ours to bear that day,
All our smiles had passed away;
Sorrow we must bear together,
Love must have its rainy weather,
Keeping still our faith in God,
As the lanes of love we trod.

Up and down the lanes of love,
Still the skies are bright above.
Feeble now we go our way,
Time has turned our hair to gray;
Rain and sunshine, joy and woe,
Both of us have come to know.
All of life's experience
Has been given us to sense;
Still our hearts keep perfect tune
As they did in days of June.

THE FIRST WATCH

If I were asked one thing to name
  Richer in pleasure's golden thrall
Which it has been my lot to claim,
  One treasure which surpasses all
The many which have made me glad—
  The greatest source of pride and joy
Would be that first real watch I had
  When I was but a little boy.

I found it at my breakfast plate
  One birthday morning years ago,
Nor have I language now to state
  The gladness of that startled: "Oh!
A watch! A real watch for me!"
  Such pleasure never comes again;
But once in life a boy can be
  So happy with a watch and chain.

The pride I felt I could not mask,
  Its ticking was a sound sublime.
I hoped that passers-by would ask
  If I could tell to them the time.

A hundred times a day, compelled
  By happy fears my play I dropped
And to my ears that watch I held
  To be convinced it hadn't stopped.

It seemed to me the world must know
  That I possessed a timepiece true;
I had a treasure I must show
  And artfully I did it, too.
I'd steal a thousand looks to see
  If still those hands were moving round,
And wondered if men noticed me
  Or heard that gentle ticking sound.

Now to that first watch here I sing
  This little feeble hymn of praise,
And all my gratitude I bring
  For radiant joy of by-gone days.
And wheresoe'er there dwells a boy,
  He, too, shall know what I have known,
And reach the topmost peak of joy
  In that first watch he soon shall own.

THE OLD HAT

To-day as I was starting out,
The lady that I write about
Stood at the door as if to chat,
Then handed me an old-time hat,
A bonnet I had worn, I know,
The first time several years ago;
"Now get this cleaned," she said to me,
"And just as good as new 'twill be."

I chuckled as I carried down
That old fedora, rusty brown.
I chuckled, living that scene o'er,
The good wife standing at the door,
As earnest as a wife can be,
Handing that worn-out lid to me,
And saying: "Have this cleaned, my dear,
'Twill serve you for another year."

Let's twist the scene around and see
What would occur if I should be
Prompted to try a trick like that
And hand to her an ancient hat,
A bonnet of a vintage rare,
Saying: "It's good enough to wear
Just have this blocked and cleaned, my dear,
'Twill serve you for another year."

I fancy then the fur would fly
If such a trick I dared to try.
She'd wither me with looks of scorn
And spoil another autumn morn.
But let it drop. A man and wife
Have different views of hats and life,
And meekly to the Greek I went
And had it cleaned—and she's content.

ENRICHED

Looking back, it seems to me
All the griefs which had to be
Left me, when the pain was o'er,
Richer than I'd been before;
And by every hurt and blow
Suffered in the Long-ago,
I can face the world to-day
In a bigger, kindlier way.

Pleasure doesn't make the man,
Life requires a sterner plan.
He who never knows a care
Never learns what he can bear;
He who never sheds a tear
Never lives through days of fear,
Has no courage he can show
When the winds of winter blow.

When the nights were dark and bleak
And in vain I'd strive to seek
Reasons for my bitter grief,
When I faltered in belief,
Little did I think or know
I should find it better so;
But to-day I've come to see
What those sorrows meant to me.

I am richer by the tears
I have shed in earlier years;
I am happier each morn
For the burdens I have borne;
And for what awaits me yet,
By the trials I have met,
I am stronger, for I know
What it means to bear a blow.

YOUTH AND THE WORLD

There is many a battle that's yet to be won,
There is many a glorious deed to be done.
The world is still young! For the youth at its door
There are tasks some shall do never dreamed of
        before.
It is not an old world, worn and wrinkled and gray,
It's a world that is being reborn every day.

The old hearts are settled and fixed and they'll do
Nothing that's daring or brilliant or new.
Their days of adventure have long since gone by,
They have finished their tasks and they're waiting
　　　to die;
But the youngsters who stand at the world's open
　　　door
Have much to achieve never dreamed of before.

On the well-traveled lanes of the land and the sea
Every day will the crowds of humanity be.
On the streets which are paved and the avenues
　　　known
Are the people who care not to venture alone.
But the young heart and stout sees the goal that's
　　　afar,
And dares to set out where the strange dangers are.

What's not possible now shall be possible when
Some young heart and brave shows the way to all
　　　men.
Youth shall remake the world. What is best of
　　　to-day
Shall to-morrow to something that's better give way.
So, come you young fellows to life, with a will,
While you work and you dream the world cannot
　　　stand still.

A PLEA

God grant me this: the right to come at night
    Back to my loved ones, head erect and true;
Beaten and bruised and from a losing fight,
    Let me be proud in what I've tried to do.

Let me come home defeated if I must,
    But clean of hands, and honor unimpaired,
Still holding firmly to my children's trust,
    Still worthy of the faith which they have shared.

God grant me this: whate'er the fates decree,
    Or do I win or lose life's little game,
I still would keep my children proud of me,
    Nor once regret that they must bear my name.

SENTIMENT

If wealth were all a man required
And all on earth to be desired,
Then he would be a fool to play
And let the dollars slip away.

If nothing mattered more than gain,
And having money ended pain,
Who'd stop at so much cash per hour
To read a book or grow a flower?

If money were the stamp of worth,
The source of fellowship and mirth,
Then he would be a fool who'd spend
The time it takes to make a friend.

But he's the fool who squanders health
And friendship's joys to pile up wealth;
Who tramples beauty down and turns
His every thought on what he earns.

For peace and joy and heart's content
Are born and bred of sentiment,
And who spends all his time for gold
Shall sigh for friends when he is old.

MY AUNT'S BONNET

They say life's simple—but I don't know.
Who can tell where a word will go?
Or how many hopes will rise and fall
With the weakest brick in the cellar wall?
Or how many hearts will break and bleed
As the result of one careless deed?
Why, my old Aunt's bonnet caused more dismay
Than a thousand suns could shine away.

She wore it high through her top-knot pinned,
A perfect kite for a heavy wind,
But the hat would stick though a gale might blow
If she found the place where the pins should go.
One Sunday morning she dressed in haste,
She hadn't a minute which she could waste,
She'd be late for church. Now the tale begins,
She didn't take care with those bonnet pins.

Oh, the wind it howled, and the wind it blew,
And away from her head that bonnet flew!
It swirled up straight to select its course,
First brushing the ears of the deacon's horse;
With a leap he scampered away in fright
And scattered the children, left and right.
A stranger grabbed for the horse's head,
But stumbled and fractured his own instead.

After the bonnet a small boy ran,
Knocked over a woman, and tripped a man.
The deacon's daughter married the chap
Who rescued her from the swaying trap,
And she lived to regret it later on.
In all that town there abided none
Whose life wasn't changed on that dreadful day
When my old Aunt's bonnet was blown away.

Some were crippled, and some went mad,
Some turned saintly, and some turned bad,
Birth and marriage and death and pain
Were all swept down in that bonnet's train.
Wives quarreled with husbands! I can't relate
The endless tricks which were played by fate.
There are folk to-day who had not been born
Had my Aunt stayed home on that Sunday morn.

THE JOY OF GETTING HOME

The joy of getting home again
  Is the sweetest thrill I know.
Though travelers by ship or train
  Are smiling when they go,
The eye is never quite so bright,
  The smile so wide and true,
As when they pass the last home light
  And all their wandering's through.

Oh, I have journeyed down to sea
  And traveled far by rail,
But naught was quite so fair to me
  As that last homeward trail.
Oh, nothing was in London town,
  Or Paris gay, or Rome
With all its splendor and renown,
  So good to see as home.

'Tis good to take these lovely trips,
  'Tis good to get away,
There's pleasure found on sailing ships,
  But travel as you may
You'll learn as most of us have learned,
  Wherever you may roam,
You're happiest when your face is turned
  Toward the lights of home.

A SUMMER DAY

Dreams are for a summer's day!
Truly rich the man who may
Let his cares and burdens shift
While his thoughts in fancy drift—
Drift and bear his soul afar
Where the long-lost splendors are.

Rich the man who for a day
Shuts the noisy world away,
Or indifferent to its urge,
Lies and sees the billows surge
On a peaceful, sunny shore,
Racing back to come once more.

Lost to fame and deaf to greed,
Feeling not the spur of need,
Freed from all the tyrants grim
Which have whipped and driven him;
There he sets his soul at large,
Drifting like a purpled barge.

Golden visions fill his eyes,
All the lust within him dies;
Beauty, from her lovely arms,
Flings to him a thousand charms,
Rich indeed the man who may
Dream away a summer day.

SHE WOULDN'T GO TO BED

Once there was a little girl who wouldn't go to bed,
Wanted to sit up all night. That is what she said.
So her pa and ma and nurse said they didn't care,
Went to bed themselves and left her sitting in her
    chair,
Left her downstairs all alone, turned out every light,
All except the one where she was sitting up all night.

Soon the house got, oh, so still and shadowy and
    queer!
This little girl who wouldn't sleep began to say:
    "Oh, dear,
I wish they hadn't gone upstairs and left me all
    alone!
I wish the wind would go away and stop that awful
    moan!
I wish the shutters wouldn't bang! I wish I hadn't
    said
I'd rather stay up all the night and never go to
    bed!"

The rocking chair dropped off to sleep, the books
    upon the shelves
Looked just as though they'd gone to bed and
    covered up themselves.
Her dolls and tea things lost their charm and grew
    too tired to play

And nothing looked as bright to her as it had look'd
     by day.
She heard the great clock ticking and she fancied
     that it said:
"It's time that little girls like you were safely tucked
     in bed."

Then up the stairs she scampered just as fast as she
     could race
And, oh, it felt so good once more to feel her
     mother's face!
And, oh, it felt so good to feel her arms and kiss her
     cheek
And snuggle down beside her and to hear her daddy
     speak!
And now I ought to tell you when the moon shines
     overhead,
I know one lovely little girl who's glad to go to bed.

SAID THE CARPENTER TO ME

"What this house is going to be,"
Said the carpenter to me,
"From the plan I cannot see.
With my hammer, saw and plane,
I can build it to remain,
Long to buffet wind and rain.

"Square the room, and strong the roof,
I can make it weather-proof,
True below and fair aloof;
But I cannot guarantee
That this house shall lovely be,
Filled with joy and sorrow-free.

"Shall these rooms with peace be filled?
Here shall anger's voice be stilled?
They must say for whom I build.
When at last I go away,
Here shall all that's tender stay?
Those who come to dwell must say.

"I have finished. Staunch the place,
Now it needs the touch of grace,

Needs a mother's smiling face,
Needs the living spirit here,
Growing lovelier year by year,
Ere this house shall glow with cheer.

"I have tried to build it well—
But shall beauty truly dwell
'Neath this roof? The years must tell.
By the tenderness displayed,
By the brave souls, unafraid,
Must this home at last be made."

HIS PHILOSOPHY

"I'm not a philosopher, bearded and gray,"
  Said he unto me.
"I'm simple of speech and I'm plain in my way,
  Which is easy to see.
I don't know the whys and the wherefores and
            whences,
What life really is and just how it commences,
But I do know the living encounter expenses.

"With high-sounding language I cannot compete,
  But some things I've learned.
I know that the money for house rent and meat
  Must always be earned.
And whether the man be day-toiler or scholar,
If his need be for coal or a tie for his collar
He must either have credit, or dig up the dollar.

"I know that I live and shall live till I die,
  And I don't have to read
Deep volumes to tell me as time hurries by
  There is much I shall need.
My problem is this: in foul weather or sunny,
My children will frequently want bread and honey
And the grocer who sells them will ask for the money.

"So having to live on the earth day by day,
   Along with the rest,
The problem's not which is the easiest way,
   But which is the best.
My philosophy's this: to look after my fences,
To think of the future before it commences
And to work for an income to meet life's expenses."

THE NEW CAR

I had an old, tired car,
   Worn with long years of travel,
A bus with many a scar
   And stained with pitch and gravel,
And all within our city
Upon the wreck took pity.

Nothing could harm it more,
   Long since was gone its splendor,
And all who looked it o'er
   With it were, oh, so tender!
Truck drivers passing there
Watched out for it with care.

And then I turned it in
   And bought a shiny new one.
Glistened its side of tin.

I'd picked a Royal blue one.
A lady in her car
Gave it its first day's jar.

I left it on the street
   In all its regal splendor,
A boy, delivering meat,
   Crumpled the forward fender.
The next day it was struck
By one who drove a truck.

Safe is the man who wears
   His face well-trimmed with plaster,
Safe seems the car that bears
   The scars of grim disaster.
But all the reckless crew
Pick on the car that's new.

THE BAD GOLFER WHO WAS GOOD

"I'm a golfer, St. Peter!" the spirit proclaimed,
"And of much I have done I am truly ashamed.
I have flubbed and I've dubbed to my pitiful cost,
But I blamed not the caddie whenever I lost.

"I've sliced and I've hooked and I've been in the
      rough,

Twenty years I've played golf, I've had trouble
  enough!
I've cursed when in sand traps, of that there's no
  doubt,
But I covered my footprints before I went out.

"I'm a golfer, St. Peter! Just one of the mutts!
My sins they are many, I've taken three putts
Countless times when I shouldn't. My record is
  black,
But always the divots I cut, I put back!

"I'm an old hundred shooter! I thought I was
  great
Whenever I finished around ninety-eight;
I was slow at the game, I confess it to you,
But I never refused to let others go through."

"Come in," said St. Peter, "come in and sit down!
Come in and I'll give you a harp and a crown!
I've a welcome for you, with the Saints you may
  dwell,
For it takes moral courage to play bad golf well."

THE MIND

The mind is that mysterious thing
Which makes the toiler and the king.
It is the realm of thought where dwells
The nursery rhymes the father tells.
It is the source of all that gives
High color to the life he lives.
It starts the smile or shapes the frown,
It lifts man up or holds him down.
It marks the happy singing lad,
It marks the neighbor kind and glad,
And world wide over this we find—
A man is fashioned by his mind.

How strange it is that what we see
And seem to cherish tenderly
Is not the outward garb of clay,
For all are formed the self-same way.
Not in the hands and legs and cheeks,
Not in the common voice which speaks,
Lies man's identity on earth—
All these come with the gift of birth.
But love and friendship and delight
Lie in a world that's hid from sight.
The mind of all is master still
To fashion them for good or ill.

So men and women here are wrought
By this strange hidden power of thought,
And each becomes in life the thing
The mind has long been fashioning.
Man's body moves and eats and drinks
And but reflects the thoughts he thinks.
His every action leaves behind
Merely the prompting of his mind.
Bad men have arms and legs and eyes.
That which we cherish or despise
And shapes each individual soul
Is wholly in the mind's control.

OUR HOUSE

I like to see a lovely lawn
Bediamoned with dew at dawn,
But mine is often trampled bare,
Because the youngsters gather there.

I like a spotless house and clean
Where many a touch of grace is seen,
But mine is often tossed about
By youngsters racing in and out.

I like a quiet house at night
Where I may sit to read and write,
But my peace flies before the tones
Of three brass throated saxophones.

My books to tumult are resigned,
In vain my furniture is shined,
My lawn is bare, my flowers fall,
Youth rides triumphant over all.

I love the grass, I love the rose,
And every living thing that grows.
I love the books I ponder o'er,
But oh, I love the children more!

And so unto myself I say:
Be mine the house where youngsters play.

Oh, little girl, oh, healthy boy,
Be mine the house which you enjoy!

HONEST PEOPLE

Life is queer and people move
Curiously along its groove.
Strange things happen now and then—
Women fair and busy men,
Led by pleasure, want or greed,
Startle us with many a deed.
Up they rise or down they fall,
Life's a puzzle to us all,
But when all is sifted out
Honor calmly walks about.

Neither wealth nor pomp nor fame
Can withstand the touch of shame.
None so clever to elude
Nature's laws of drink or food,
None so smart that he can break
Nature's laws for pleasure's sake.
Life, with all its curious turns,
Soon the shrewd observer learns,
Howsoe'er his battles cease,
Leaves the honest man in peace.

Life is queer, but gentle ways
Win the world's unstinted praise,
Sin and shame and vice are here,
Taking toll from year to year;
But the brave heart and the true
Need not fear what they may do,
And the clean of heart and hand
All these terrors can withstand;
For when all is sifted out
Honor calmly walks about.

THE FIRST EASTER

Dead they left Him in the tomb
And the impenetrable gloom,
Rolled the great stone to the door,
Dead, they thought, forevermore.

Then came Mary Magdalene
Weeping to that bitter scene,
And she found, to her dismay,
That the stone was rolled away.

Cometh Peter then and John,
Him they'd loved to look upon,
And they found His linen there
Left within the sepulchre.

"They have taken Him away!"
Mary cried that Easter Day.
Low, she heard a voice behind:
"Whom is it you seek to find?"

"Tell me where He is!" she cried,
"Him they scourged and crucified.
Here we left Him with the dead!"
"Mary! Mary!" Jesus said.

So by Mary Magdalene
First the risen Christ was seen,
And from every heart that day
Doubt's great stone was rolled away.

THE MISSING MAN

There was a man I once knew well,
Who had no stocks and bonds to sell;
  No subdivided acres which
  In seven years would make me rich;
No sets of books to fill my mind
With knowledge of the deeper kind;
No self-improvement courses in
The mystery of how to win.
Whene'er he called it was to say:
"Well, how are all your folks to-day?"

I wonder where this man has flown?
I wish he'd make his presence known.
  Whene'er he came to visit me,
  He asked no gift for charity,
He never asked me to subscribe
To funds to feed an Indian tribe,
Or carry on deep sea research
Or lift the mortgage on his church.
  Whene'er he called it was to chat
  In fellowship of this and that.

I watch to see him pass my door,
But unto me he comes no more,
  For every caller now I find
  Has dotted lines he wishes signed.
Oh, good old friend! I fancy you

Suspect that I have work to do,
And that is why you stay away,
But come again to me, I pray,
    That I may say: "Well, after all,
    One man still pays a friendly call."

FOR FISH AND BIRDS

For fish and birds I make this plea,
May they be here long after me,
May those who follow hear the call
Of old Bob White in spring and fall;
And may they share the joy that's mine
When there's a bass upon the line.

I found the world a wondrous place.
A cold wind blowing in my face
Has brought the wild ducks in from sea;
God grant the day shall never be
When youth upon November's shore
Shall see the mallards come no more!

I found the world a garden spot.
God grant the desolating shot
And barbed hook shall not destroy
Some future generation's joy!
Too barren were the earth for words
If gone were all the fish and birds.

Fancy an age that sees no more
The mallards winging into shore;
Fancy a youth with all his dreams
That finds no fish within the streams.
Our world with life is wondrous fair,
God grant we do not strip it bare!

MY LIFE

I have a life I can't escape,
  A life that's mine to mold and shape,
Some things I lack of strength and skill,
  I blunder much and fumble; still
I can in my own way design
  What is to be this life of mine.

It is not mine to say how much
  Of gold and silver I shall clutch,
What heights of glory I shall climb,
  What splendid deeds achieve in time;
Lacking the genius of the great
  The lesser tasks may be my fate.

But I can say what I shall be,
What in my life the world shall see;
Can mold my thoughts and actions here

To what is fine or what is drear.
Though small my skill, I can elect
To keep or lose my self-respect.

No man can kindlier be than I,
No man can more detest a lie,
I can be just as clean and true
As any gifted genius, who
Rises to earthly heights of fame
And wins at last the world's acclaim.

I can be friendly, blithe of heart,
Can build or tear my life apart,
Can happy-natured smile along
And shrug my shoulders at a wrong.
I only choose what is to be
This life which symbolizes me.

MERIT AND THE THRONG

A thousand men filed in by day
To work and later draw their pay;
A thousand men with hopes and dreams,
Ambitions, visions, plans and schemes.
And in the line a youth who said:
"What chance have I to get ahead?
In such a throng, can any tell
Whether or not I labor well?"

Yet merit is so rare a trait
That once it enters by the gate,
Although 'tis mingled with the throng,
The news of it is passed along.
A workman sees a willing boy,
And talks about his find with joy;
A foreman hears the word, and seeks
The lad of whom another speaks.

So up the line the news is passed,
And to the chief it comes at last.
A willing ear to praise he lends,
Then for that eager boy he sends
And gives him little tasks to do
To learn if all that's said be true.
Among the throng the lad is one
He keeps a watchful eye upon.

Oh, youngster, walking with the throng,
Although to-day the road seems long,
Remember that it lies with you
To say what kind of work you'll do.
If you are only passing fair
The chief will never know you're there,
But if you've merit, have no doubt,
The chief will quickly find it out.

THE WASTER

Oh, the days I've wasted, the days I've had to spend
And tossed away to serve a whim, as if they'd have
    no end.
Old Father Time can tell you that I'm a wayward
    son,
I've had a dozen fortunes and gone through every
    one.

I should have turned the grindstone when steel
    required an edge,
But summer birds were singing upon my window
    ledge.
I should have strung together small words to make
    a rhyme,
But summer is for playing and work for winter-
    time.

They tell me time is money, and well I know that's
      true,
But who would be a rich man when skies above are
      blue?
And I have turned from toiling a game of golf to
      shoot,
And what its cost in silver I wouldn't dare compute.

A slave to fame and fortune I have no wish to be,
There are a thousand splendors on earth I want to
      see.
A dreamer and a waster I've laughed my way along
Indifferent to fortune, but tempted by a song.

CHECKING THE DAY

I had a full day in my purse
    When I arose, and now it's gone!
I wonder if I can rehearse
    The squandered hours, one by one,
And count the minutes as I do
    The pennies and the dimes I've spent.
I've had a day, once bright and new,
    But, oh, for what few things it went!

There were twelve hours when I began,
    Good hours worth sixty minutes each,
Yet some of them so swiftly ran
    I had no time for thought or speech.

Eight of them to my task I gave,
  Glad that it did not ask for more.
Part of the day I tried to save,
  But now I cannot say what for.

An hour I spent for idle chat,
  Gossip and scandal I confess;
No better off am I for that,
  Would I had talked a little less.
I watched steel workers bolt a beam,
  What time that cost I don't recall.
How very short the minutes seem
  When they are spent on trifles small.

Quite empty is my purse to-night
  Which held at dawn a twelve-hour day,
For all of it has taken flight—
  Part wisely spent, part thrown away.
I did my task and earned its gain,
  But checking deeds with what they cost,
Two missing hours I can't explain,
  They must be charged away as lost.

TWO WORLDS

There are two worlds wherein to dwell,
  And one is harsh and stern;
The other lies where none can tell
  And none can ever learn,
For each man keeps a secret place
To meet his spirit face to face.

The world of fact is known to all,
  Its streets are paved and hard
And lined with buildings cold and tall
  And some with windows barred.
There fame and fortune are the gods
Which set the stakes and make the odds.

And what a man is there is not
  The man he'd like to be,
For there the pace is swift and hot,
  In constant strife is he.
Men judge him for the thing he seems
Who never finds his world of dreams.

But in that shadowy vale of thought,
  To which at times he flees,
He finds the peace he long has sought
  And endless beauty sees.
In silence with his dreams he dwells
Where no one either buys or sells.

ON CHURCH BUILDING

God builds no churches! By His plan,
That labor has been left to man.
No spires miraculously rise,
No little mission from the skies
Falls on a bleak and barren place
To be a source of strength and grace.
The humblest church demands its price
In human toil and sacrifice.

Men call the church the House of God,
Towards which the toil stained pilgrims plod
In search of strength and rest and hope,
As blindly through life's mists they grope,
And there God dwells, but it is man
Who builds that house and draws its plan;
Pays for the mortar and the stone
That none need seek for God alone.

There is no church but what proclaims
The gifts of countless generous names.
Ages before us spires were raised
'Neath which Almighty God was praised
As proof that He was then, as now.
Those sacred altars, where men bow
Their heads in prayer and sorrow lifts
Its heavy weight, are Christian gifts!

The humblest spire in mortal ken,
Where God abides, was built by men.
And if the church is still to grow,
Is still the light of hope to throw
Across the valleys of despair,
Men still must build God's house of prayer.
God sends no churches from the skies,
Out of our hearts must they arise!

A FEW NEW TEETH

The dentist tinkered day by day,
  With wax and sticky gum;
He built a model out of clay
  And shaped it with his thumb.
He made the man a lovely plate,
  With three teeth in a row,
And bars of gold to keep them straight,
  Then said: "They'll never show.

"Go forth," the dentist told the man,
  "As proud as you can be.
Those teeth are perfect. No one can
  Tell they were bought from me.
Why I, by whom the work was wrought,
  The truth had never known.
Were you a stranger I'd have thought
  Those teeth were all your own."

While going out he bumped a miss.
　　"Excuthe me pleathe," he said.
The lady smiled to hear him hiss—
　　His cheeks went flaming red.
He met a friend upon the street,
　　Who joined him for a walk
And said: "Let's go where we can eat,
　　And have a quiet talk."

"I'd rather walk," the man exclaimed.
　　"Leth thtay upon the threet,
For with you I thould be athamed
　　Thum tholid food to eat."
"New teeth?" the friend remarked, and low
　　The troubled man said: "Yeth!
My dentith thwore you'd never know.
　　However did you guetth?"

BRIDE AND GROOM

Oh, bride and groom, the day is fair
And love is singing everywhere!
And friends are many, smiling now
The while you take your marriage vow;
But life is made of joy and care
And love has many things to bear.

God bless the home which you shall build!
May it with happiness be filled,
May you set forth this lovely June
To many a golden honeymoon;
But storms will come, as old hearts know,
And love must weather many a blow.

Go hand in hand adown the years,
Keep faith through doubts and hurts and tears,
The honeymoon will rise and wane,
Joy will be lost and found again;
The tears must come to every eye,
But love can live when hope must die.

Oh, bride and groom, for you my prayer
Is not that every day be fair,
For that could never be. I pray
That love shall last, whate'er the day;
Through all that comes of grief and pain
And hurt and care may love remain.

FISHERMAN'S LUCK

I can be happy in a boat
  And watch the clouds go by.
My collar open at the throat
  Unfettered by a tie,
And while I like the fish to bite
  And long to have a string,
I do not grumble much at night
  If I don't catch a thing.

And so I merely set it down
  To illustrate my luck,
When I desert the busy town
  To fish, I've never struck
The happy day I hear about,
  So fortunate and fair,
When all the boys were taking out
  The law's allotment there.

"Oh, happy yesterday!" they cry,
  "The fish were running strong!"
To-day there is too bright a sky
  Or something else is wrong.
I know the fish are here. I'm told
  So many wondrous tales,
But here to-day the wind blows cold
  And all my casting fails.

Now I am back in town once more
    And now the natives write:
"To-day we landed twenty-four!
    You should have felt them bite!"
But vain it is for me to wish.
    Luck always turns me down,
I always seem to fish for fish
    That bite when I'm in town.

FATE TALKS ABOUT MEN

Into my room a stranger came,
    Coarse and rough and a thing to hate,
And I, half-frightened, inquired his name,
    Said he with a laugh: "I'm known as Fate."
"Oh!" I answered. "Then you're the man,
Who blocks full many a well-laid plan.

"You made a loafer of one I knew,
    At least he says that the fault is yours.
You made a thief of another, who
    Now spends the years behind prison doors.
There's many a pitiful thing of shame,
Who sits and sighs and reviles your name."

"Yes, I get blamed for a lot of things,"
    Said Fate, with a twinkle in his eye,
"When men must hear what their folly brings
    I'm the handiest sort of an alibi.
Harsh things of me may the failures think,
But I never have asked a man to drink.

"I never have asked a man to lie.
    I've spilled his dream and I've spoiled his plan,
You see it's my business on earth to try
    The moral courage of every man.
I'm a troublesome sort of a chap to meet,
But I've never suggested that man should cheat.

"I hit men hard and I hurt at times.
    I cause them trouble, I will agree,
But the fellows who put their hands to crimes
    Don't get that sort of a jolt from me.
Men say I'm the cause of a lot of shame,
But in most of the cases I'm not to blame."

NO HONEY-GATHERER

When the bees are in the clover,
And a blue sky's bending over
This old world, aglow with sunshine
Just as far as I can see;
When the breezes are suggesting
All the happiness of resting,
Though it's time to gather honey
Then I'm glad I'm not a bee.

There are some who flit for money
As the bee goes after honey,
There are splendors all around them
Which they never pause to see.
They are slaves to Tyrant Duty,
But when summer spills her beauty
And makes days as fair as this one
Then I'm glad I'm not a bee.

Oh! I think it is much better
Not to be a honey-getter,
I would rather lie and dream here
Underneath this shady tree.
Let the busy bee keep working,
Here's a day just made for shirking,
In this lovely summer weather
I don't want to be a bee.

THE OLD SAILOR TALKS

There was action in the old days when I learned to
love the sea,
There was beauty in the canvas which your turbines
can't replace.
Oh, the liner is a lady! But she's not the girl for me,
For she's business-like and snappy and there's
hardness in her face,
And I like to see my woman wear a little bit of lace.

There was poetry in sailing when the seas were
running free,
There was music in the rigging when the wind
began to blow,
But the liner, she is haughty, and she's not the girl
for me,
She walks away from humble ships who try to say
"hello!"
And I like to have my woman sort o' friendly, don't
you know.

It's all business now, in sailing, as I think you will
agree,
With arrivals and departures just as regular as bed.
Oh, the liner is a lady! But she's not the girl for me,
She always shows about the same each time the
log is read,
And I'd rather have a woman with some nonsense
in her head.

EQUIPMENT

Figure it out for yourself, my lad,
You've all that the greatest of men have had,
Two arms, two hands, two legs, two eyes,
And a brain to use if you would be wise.
With this equipment they all began,
So start for the top and say, "I can."

Look them over, the wise and great,
They take their food from a common plate,
And similar knives and forks they use,
With similar laces they tie their shoes,
The world considers them brave and smart,
But you've all they had when they made their start.

You can triumph and come to skill,
You can be great if you only will.
You're well equipped for what fight you choose,
You have legs and arms and a brain to use,
And the man who has risen great deeds to do,
Began his life with no more than you.

You are the handicap you must face,
You are the one who must choose your place,
You must say where you want to go,
How much you will study the truth to know.
God has equipped you for life, but He
Lets you decide what you want to be.

Courage must come from the soul within,
The man must furnish the will to win.
So figure it out for yourself, my lad,
You were born with all that the great have had,
With your equipment they all began.
Get hold of yourself, and say: "I can."

AUNT JANE WORRIED

Aunt Jane was one of the worrying kind,
Early and late with a troubled mind
Fearing the worst, in her chair she sat
Grieving herself over this and that.

Aunt Jane's particular stock in trade
Was things of which she could be afraid.
There wasn't a horror of which she'd read
That ever escaped from her shaking head.

Murder, robbery, death at sea,
Troubled and frightened her terribly.
Every possible evil which may occur
Was a terrible thing which might happen to her.

She feared death by trolleys, and death by fire,
Nothing but bad news came by wire,
And the curious thing about my Aunt Jane
Is all that she gathered from life was pain.

It never occurred to her once to think
That thousands of steamers at sea don't sink.
By a horrible fate was her life accurst,
She was doomed forever to fear the worst.

Never she looked to receive the best,
Always by gloom was her mind impressed;
And at last death ended life's frightful round,
But not once was she murdered, or robbed, or
        drowned.

THE GENTLE MAN

His life was gentle, and his mind
The little splendors seemed to find.
   The baser side of life he saw,
   But from the blemish and the flaw
He turned, as if he understood
That none of us is wholly good.

He lived as one who seemed to know
That as the swift days come and go
   Clouds blanket skies that should be fair,
   Rain is encountered everywhere,
And so o'er every human form
Must blow at times the bitter storm.

As one who loves a garden, he
Walked round the world its charms to see.
   Not only by the rose he stayed,
   The tiniest violet in the shade
On his devotion could depend,
To great and low he played the friend.

And as the gardener seems to give
More care to plants which fight to live
   So he, with tenderer regard,
   Befriended those whose tasks were hard.
Thus dealing gently, he became
More than a high and haughty name.

This was his wealth, that good and bad
Of him some happy memory had.
   This was his fame, that high and low
   Their love for him were proud to show.
This his success, that at the end
Men mourned the passing of a friend.

IF TO BE CLEVER

If to be clever means that I must sneer
   At every honest effort to be good,
Must tear to pieces all the brave revere,
   And scorn what isn't clearly understood;
If only what is rotten can be art,
Lord, keep me from the sin of being smart!

If to be clever means that I must jest
   At all that men hold sacred, and disdain
The simple teachings telling what is best,
   Must serve the passions for my pocket's gain;
If brilliance means an utter lack of heart,
Lord, save me from the sin of being smart!

If to be clever means that I must see
   All that is base and vile and call that real,
And finding honor, swear it cannot be
   Because I've known some men to lie and steal;
If wit must tear all gentle worth apart,
Lord, save me from the sin of being smart!

GRACE

Dear Lord, for food and drink and peace
    And all that makes our day so fair,
And for the evening's sweet release
    From duty and its round of care
Once more we turn to Thee above,
Acknowledging Thy boundless love.

Be with us through this night, we pray,
    And make our little circle strong;
May none among us go astray.
    Help us to choose the right from wrong.
Within these walls, however tried,
May love and friendliness abide.

Dear Lord, in every blossoming tree,
    In every bloom our garden knows
Thy marvelous handiwork we see,
    Thy love we find in every rose.
Lord, may the service which is ours
Reflect Thy glory as the flowers.

DREAMS

One broken dream is not the end of dreaming,
   One shattered hope is not the end of all,
Beyond the storm and tempest stars are gleaming,
   Still build your castles, though your castles fall.

Though many dreams come tumbling in disaster,
   And pain and heartache meet us down the years,
Still keep your faith, your dreams and hopes to
      master
   And seek to find the lesson of your tears.

Not all is as it should be! See how littered
   With sorry wreckage is life's restless stream.
Some dreams are vain, but be you not embittered
   And never cry that you have ceased to dream!

"I DIDN'T THINK AND I FORGOT"

The weakest excuses of all the lot
Are: "I didn't think" and "I forgot."
Worn and weary and haggard and pale,
They follow the path of the men who fail—
In thread-bare raiment from place to place
They've dogged the steps of the human race.
In most of the blunders which men have made
This pitiful pair a part have played.

A man cries out on disaster's brink:
"I should have stopped but I didn't think!"
Was the barn door locked last night? 'Twas not.
And somebody mutters: "Oh, I forgot!"
Since Adam and Eve and the world began,
This pair have followed the trail of man.
The commonest phrases in printer's ink
Are "I forgot" and "I didn't think."

Yet man will think if a pleasure calls,
And there isn't a doubt that he recalls
The promise another has made to him;
And a boy will think that he wants to swim,
And the chances are that he won't forget
That he mustn't come home with his hair all wet.
It's strange, but duty is all I find
That ever escapes from a failure's mind.

Search the burdens which men must bear
And you'll find the tracks of this precious pair.
With needless trouble this world they've filled,
And who can measure the tears they've spilled?
"I forgot" has wrecked ship and train,
"I didn't think" has caused endless pain,
And God must smile, as He sees us sink,
At our "I forgot" and "I didn't think."

GIANT STORIES

One time I told a giant tale before she went to bed,
But now when evening comes I tell her fairy tales
        instead,
  "A story shouldn't frighten her,
  It really ought to brighten her,
You should have been ashamed to talk of giants,"
        Mother said.

This giant had an ugly face with whiskers just like
        wire,
He lived upon a mountain top, and kept a blazing
        fire
  And so one night I chaptered him.
  And told her how they captured him—
A story not just suitable when little girls retire.

For in the night she woke and shrieked and shouted
     loud for me.
And what the trouble was, of course, I hurried in
     to see,
  "The giant came in here!" she said,
  "His ugly face was near," she said,
An awful dream, which Mother says should never,
     never be.

So fairy tales at night I tell, of pretty hills and dales,
Of dances up and down the hills and on the blossomy
     trails.
  I know I mustn't frighten her,
  And so I try to brighten her,
But strange to say that little miss still begs for giant
     tales!

THE HARD JOB

It's good to do the hard job, for it's good to play the
      man,
For the hard job strengthens courage which the
      easy never can,
And the hard job, when it's over, gives the man a
      broader smile—
For it brings the joy of knowing that he's done a
      thing worth while.

Oh, stand you to your hard job with the will to see
      it through,
Be glad that you can face it and be glad it's yours
      to do;
It is when the task is mighty and the outcome deep
      in doubt,
The richest joys are waiting for the man who'll work
      it out.

Beyond the gloom of failure lies the glory to be
      won,
When the hard job is accomplished and the doubtful
      task is done;
For it's manhood in the making and its courage put
      to test—
So buckle to the hard job—it's your chance to do
      your best.

LIFE'S NEEDS

Oh, let me have my work to do,
A book to read for an hour or two;
A garden, for an outside room,
Where little things I've planted bloom;
A dog to follow at my heels;
My children's laughter at my meals,
And love to greet me at the door,
And I'll not ask this world for more.

Just grant me strength to face the day;
The wit a grown man's part to play;
A few good friends my lot to share;
A suit of clothes that's fit to wear;
A good night's rest when day is done;
The zest for sport, the taste for fun;
An eye for all that's fair to see,
And full contented I shall be.

No climber I, who would ascend
Beyond the reach of last year's friends.
Give me a few things such as these:
Companionship with flowers and trees,
And summer's birds; the faith to bear
Whate'er of sorrow is my share;
And love to last till life is o'er,
And I'll not ask the world for more.

SEA-DREAMS

I never see a gallant ship go steaming out to sea,
But what a little boy who was comes running back
  to me,
A little chap I thought was dead or lost forevermore,
Who used to watch the ships go out and long to quit
  the shore.

He followed them to India, to China and Japan,
He told the flying sea gulls that he'd be a sailor-man.
"Some day," he said, "I'll own a ship and sail to
  Singapore,
And maybe bring a parrot back, or two or three or
  four."

And often when he went to bed, this little boy would
  lie
And fancy that the ceiling was a wide and starry sky;
The ocean was beneath him, and as happy as could be
He was master of a vessel that was putting out to sea.

But something happened to the lad, and now he is no
  more,
For in his place there is a man who never leaves the
  shore;
I often think of him as dead, but back he comes to me
Whene'er I see a gallant ship go steaming out to sea.

THE TRAGEDIES OF INNOCENCE

When sages old on life reflect,
'Tis strange they seldom recollect
The floods of tears which daily rise
In countless little children's eyes,
But see upon life's moving stage
Only the tragedies of age.

Yet innocence is prey to grief
Unsoothed by any firm belief.
To-day her favorite doll she dropped,
Her little heart in terror stopped,
And with the crash the sunshine fled
Because her lovely child was dead.

That stab of anguish was as real
As any shock which grown-ups feel.
Age could not sorrow plainer speak
Than those great tears upon her cheek.
The day her lovely goldfish died
The whole night long she sobbed and cried.

Say not that hurt and loss and care
Are only for the old to bear.
For each must suffer in his turn
Since life to one and all is stern.
And scenes on which old age has smiled
Were bitter sorrows to a child.

TEAM WORK

It's all very well to have courage and skill
    And it's fine to be counted a star,
But the single deed with its touch of thrill
    Doesn't tell us the man you are;
For there's no lone hand in the game we play,
    We must work to a bigger scheme,
And the thing that counts in the world to-day
    Is, How do you pull with the team?

They may sound your praise and call you great,
    They may single you out for fame,
But you must work with your running mate
    Or you'll never win the game;
Oh, never the work of life is done
    By the man with a selfish dream,
For the battle is lost or the battle is won
    By the spirit of the team.

You may think it fine to be praised for skill,
    But a greater thing to do
Is to set your mind and set your will
    On the goal that's just in view;
It's helping your fellowman to score
    When his chances hopeless seem;
It's forgetting self till the game is o'er
    And fighting for the team.

HAD YOUTH BEEN WILLING TO LISTEN

If youth had been willing to listen
  To all that its grandfathers told,
If the gray-bearded sage by the weight of his age
  Had been able attention to hold,
We'd be reading by candles and heating with wood,
And where we were then we'd have certainly stood.

If youth had been willing to listen
  To the warnings and hints of the wise,
Had it taken as true all the best which they knew,
  And believed that no higher we'd rise,
The windows of sick rooms would still be kept shut
And we'd still use a cobweb to bandage a cut.

If youth had been willing to listen,
  Had it clung to the best of the past,
With oxen right now we'd be struggling to plough
  And thinking a horse travels fast.
We'd have stood where we were beyond question
    or doubt
If some pestilent germ hadn't wiped us all out.

So, although I am gray at the temples,
  And settled and fixed in my ways,
I wouldn't hold youth to the limits of truth
  That I learned in my brief yesterdays.
And I say to myself as they come and they go:
"Those kids may find something this age doesn't
    know."

THE CANDY-MAN

All-day suckers and lollypops,
Maple fudges and chocolate drops!
Wares that satisfy; goods that please!
Who sells lovelier things than these?
Who, among all of our working clan,
Has a happier trade than the candy-man?

Peppermint sticks and nougat bars!
Lemon and strawberry drops in jars!
Where on the earth is a job which beats
The glorious business of selling sweets?
Here is a salesman who satisfies
And gladdens the heart of the one who buys.

All day long the children race
With shouts of glee to his tempting place;
Never a customer cross appears,
Laughter is all that he ever hears.
Friendship is all that he ever meets—
For he's in the business of selling sweets.

If I were starting my life again,
I wouldn't be slave to a faulty pen,
I wouldn't barter life's joy for fame,
But over a shop I would nail my name;
I'd be the candy man, proud to tell
That I had nothing but sweets to sell.

STUDY THE RULES

Oh, whether it's business or whether it's sport,
  Study the rules.
Know every one of them, long and the short.
  Study the rules.
Know what you may do, and what you may not.
Know what your rights are. 'Twill help you a lot
In the critical times when the battle is hot.
  Study the rules.

Life's not a scramble, and sport's not a mess.
  Study the rules.
Nothing is left to haphazard or guess.
  Study the rules.
Know what's a foul blow, and what is a fair;
Know all the penalties recognized there;
Know what to go for, and what to beware.
  Study the rules.

Nature has fixed for us definite laws.
  Study the rules!
Every effect is the child of a cause.
  Study the rules.
Nature has penalties she will inflict,
When it comes to enforcing them nature is strict.
Her eyes are wide open. She never is tricked.
  Study the rules.

Play to your best in the game as it's played.
    Study the rules.
Know how a fair reputation is made.
    Study the rules.
Sport has a standard, and life has a plan—
Don't go at them blindly; learn all that you can—
Know all that is asked and required of a man.
    Study the rules!

THE BATTERED DREAM SHIP

Oh, once I sent a ship to sea, and Hope was on
        her bow,
But Time has brought her back to me and Wis-
        dom's painted now;
Yes, Time has brought me many things and some
        of them were good,
And some of them were failure's stings I little
        understood.

When Hope set forth the dream was fair, the sea
        was calm and blue,
I knew men met with storms out there and had to
        ride them through;
But still I dreamed my ship would ride and weather
        every blow,
For Hope flings many a truth aside which Wisdom
        comes to know.

The storms have come with bitter cold, I've prayed
        unto the Lord,
I've had false cargoes in the hold and thrown them
        overboard;
I've trimmed my sails to meet the gale, I've cut my
        journey short;
With battered hulk and tattered sail at last I've
        come to port.

'Tis not enough to hope and dream, for storms will
        surely rise,
However smooth the sea may seem, 'tis there dis-
        aster lies;
And I have learned from time and stress, that those
        who ride the wave
And come at last to happiness must suffer and be
        brave.

THE HOME TOWN

It doesn't matter much be its buildings great or
     small,
The home town, the home town is the best town,
     after all.
The cities of the millions have the sun and stars
     above,
But they lack the friendly faces of the few you've
     learned to love,
And with all their pomp of riches and with all their
     teeming throngs,
The heart of man is rooted in the town where he
     belongs.

There are places good to visit, there are cities fair
     to see,
There are haunts of charm and beauty where at
     times it's good to be,
But the humblest little hamlet sings a melody to
     some,
And no matter where they travel it is calling them
     to come;
Though cities rise to greatness and are gay with
     gaudy dress,
There is something in the home town which no other
     towns possess.
The home town has a treasure which the distance
     cannot gain,

It is there the hearts are kindest, there the gentlest
     friends remain;
It is there a mystic something seems to permeate
     the air
To set the weary wanderer to wishing he were
     there;
And be it great or humble, it still holds mankind
     in thrall,
For the home town, the home town, is the best town
     after all.

BENEATH THE STARS

Beneath the stars at night when all was clear,
  We sat and talked and wondered how and when
 The truth first broke within the sight of men;
What was it set them dreaming, thinking here;
Led them to hope and struggle year by year,
  To turn their backs upon the cave man's den;
  See order here and beauty's charm and then
Discover God where all seemed bleak and drear.

"They must have felt within themselves," one said,
"The spark eternal and the fire divine;
They must have heard God whispering overhead
  On nights like this with every star ashine."
And all agreed that man began to rise
When first he sensed the splendor of the skies.

PERILS OF A PUBLIC SPEAKER

A public speaker's lot is not an easy one to bear,
There's many a slip twixt thought and lip which
      takes him unaware,
For the ablest chap will meet a trap he never
      dreamed was there.

From year to year uncounted queer and startling
      things have sprung
All unforeseen, where I have been, to trip my halt-
      ing tongue;
I've stood in state, compelled to wait, while parents
      spanked their young.

But last July, I'll vow that I met my extremest fate,
In church I stood, with all the good, a moment to
      orate,
With one brave swoop I looped the loop with their
      collection plate.

I did not know it stood below and just within my
      reach,
My only thought was what I ought to mention in
      my speech.
I flicked my hand. You understand, that gesture
      was a peach!

Direct and straight I caught that plate beneath its
  velvet chin,
The nickels flew as nickels do, the dimes went roll-
  ing in
The furnace pipe. Oh, cruel swipe, which started
  such a din!

That goodly coin went down to join perdition's
  blazing coals,
While much concerned I stood and learned how far
  a quarter rolls.
I lost the speech, designed to reach those panting,
  thirsty souls.

With one fell crash, I knocked that cash right back
  from whence it came;
The parson sighed, the warden cried, my cheeks
  grew red with shame.
The children fought for dimes. They thought it
  was a scrambling game.

At times I've had some moments sad, some cruel
  pranks of fate,
But never quite so grim a plight, I venture now to
  state,
As when in church, from off its perch, I knocked
  that money plate.

A HINT

My son, when plans have gone astray
   And careless blunders bring
The crash which spoils your hopeful day
   Or failure's bitter sting,
Remember, as you face despair,
The dullest fool knows how to swear.

When things go wrong, as oft they will,
   Don't let your passions go;
Remember signs of temper ill
   The dullest mind can show.
It's proof of neither strength nor brains
To whine too loudly at your pains.

An idiot can curse and swear,
   A dolt can rave and shriek,
But oft it calls for courage rare
   No angry word to speak.
Fools are proficiently profane.
Who would stay cool must have a brain.

THE DUB GOLFER

I'm the sensitive soul that is known as the dub!
I'm the fellow that's shunned by the boys at the
     club.
  On the course I am slow,
    And I get in the way.
  There is much I don't know
    About golf, I may say.
I'm supposed to stand by when good golfers shout
     "fore!"
And if I refuse all the members get sore.
I'm never considered when matches are made,
But my bill always comes when the dues must be
     paid.

I'm laughed at by youngsters who drive straight and
     far.
I'm jeered at by boys who can shoot holes at par.
  I'm a dub at the game
    And I just plod along,
  But I'll add, just the same,
    That I'm one of a throng.
We may not be much in the tournament play,
We may clog up the course in our pitiful way;
We're not wanted out there, but they never forget
To assess us whenever they've run into debt.

I'm a dub with the many; despised by the few.
Old Hundred's the best I can possibly do.

But I notice when they
   Post the names at the club
Of the boys who don't pay,
   There is seldom a dub.
It's often the wonderful golfer who's short,
The fellow who shouts we've no place in the sport.
And I shudder to think what the clubs would be
   like
If we dubs got together and went on a strike.

INDIVIDUALITY

Some say that chance or guess or hazard makes
   The things we grow to be. That unto earth
   We're plunged like plummets in the hour of birth
To find our places when cold reason wakes;
To crawl and stumble through our own mistakes
   And blindly seek for comfort and for mirth;
That on the path where one man proves his worth
Another with the self-same courage breaks.

I think there is a time which comes to all
   When each must see his life a perfect whole;
Must feel that he, in some way, large or small,
   Is shaping, not a fortune, but a soul.
That in the end, in spite of all mistakes,
His worth is fashioned by the choice he makes.

STYLE

I've never worn a high silk hat,
    I've never borne a cane,
And to the gray pearl-buttoned spat
    Indifferent I remain.

I do not quarrel with the men
    Who wear these things with grace,
Spats now are seen on nine in ten
    Until they're commonplace.

And men there are can walk the street
    En route to church or not,
And seem at ease, to all they meet,
    Beneath a chimney pot.

And some there are can swing a cane
    With masters of the art,
But I forever must remain
    Outside the very smart.

For if I owned a high silk hat
    I'd leave it on the shelf,
Beneath a glistening lid like that
    I'd have to laugh myself.

And if in spats I walked about
    Uneasy I would be,

Expecting everyone to shout
　　Derisively at me.

And so I watch the men who wear
　　The nobby things so well
And wonder how it is they dare
　　To be so very swell.

I see them in their Sunday best
　　Stroll easily about,
But were I dressed as they are dressed
　　I'd never venture out.

GARDENERS

Shame seldom gets the man who sees
Beauty in growing plants and trees.
Who keeps a garden trim and fair
Has little time for sin to spare.
Who loves to work among the flowers
Has many a task for idle hours.

Love lingers where the roses grow.
The men and women who bestow
Some time on poppies, pansies, phlox,
And give their thought to hollyhocks,
And learn to know them all by name,
Will seldom blunder into shame.

Who loves a little garden place
Can laugh temptation in the face.
The flowers which are his joy and pride
Will keep him gladly occupied,
For he will give to beauty fair
Whatever time he has to spare.

I never see a garden small,
With morning glories on the wall
And little blooms, but what I say
Here is a home that's built to stay.
Here dwell, with fern and mignonette,
Good people shame will never get.

THE FINE ARTS

Give us more lovers of beauty,
    More lovers of gardens, and we
Shall lessen our need for your cannon
    And iron-clad ships of the sea.

Give us more lovers of music,
    More lovers of pictures and books,
And we'll fill up the world with good neighbors
    And dwindle the number of crooks.

For hatred and malice and scheming
    And envy and cunning and greed
And all that makes crime a temptation
    Are not in an art lover's creed.

Who gives his attention to beauty,
    Who cherishes laughter and song,
And is thrilled by the glory of planets,
    Not often another will wrong.

In gardens, in childhood, in painting,
    In music are safety and peace,
So give us more lovers of beauty
    That hatred and quarrels may cease.

POSSESSION

The woods and fields and trees are ours
With all their lavish wealth of flowers;
The stars at night which brightly shine,
The morning sun, are yours and mine;
And added to such joys as these
We stand possessors of the breeze.

Who calls us poor, because we lack
The nation's printed yellow-back,
Is only partly right. We share
God's mercy with the millionaire.
No more of beauty can he see
Than that which smiles at you and me.

We own the earth for all our time.
Wherever summer roses climb
For us to gaze on, they are ours.
Where'er a snow-capped mountain towers
We've but to turn our heads to say,
That splendid thing is ours to-day.

To us the blue of Heaven belongs.
Ours are the wild birds' merry songs.
Silver and gold are scarce, but oh,
What countless charms the days bestow!
And here, right at our humble doors,
Of splendor we have endless stores.

THE WISE

Some look at care as if it should not be,
  As if mishaps to them should never fall;
Though hurt and pain must come to you and me
  They should know life and never wince at all.

What strange philosophy is this which sees
  The tears of grief fill up a neighbor's eyes
And says: "I shall be spared such agonies;
  My babe shall live, though many another dies?"

Thus blinded to life's facts most common-place,
  Some sing and dance and spend their little wage.
Then comes the day they have a loss to face
  And bitterly they fly into a rage.

Having no strength for trouble and no wit,
  These self-deluded persons turn and flee.
How could they face a blow, prepared for it,
  Who have not thought that such a thing must be?

Wiser are they who know how close are tears,
  How near is trouble in its various shapes.
They build a wall of faith against their fears
  And plan for hurts from which no one escapes.

"I played so badly," said the organist,
    "I'm thankful but a few
Came here to-night through all the fog and mist
    To hear me through.

"My fingers seemed to fumble with the keys
    As if they, too, were proud
And would not bend a little, just to please
    So small and poor a crowd."

And saying this, he left the cold, dim hall;
    But one there was who stayed,
Still lingering, as if trying to recall
    Some melody he'd played.

"How glorious it was!" she said to me.
    "What matters rain,
When one by music can uplifted be
    Above all pain?"

And so I set this down in hope that he
    May learn and smile,
Finding that work, which poor he deemed to be,
    Was still worth while.

DEATH, THE COLLECTOR

Death, the collector, came to him and said:
"I want the payment for your drink and bread!
I want the price which tenants all must pay
For having occupied a house of clay.
This is a bill which cannot be denied."
"Please call another time," the man replied.

"I'm sorry, but to-day I'm not prepared.
I really thought your master little cared
How long this lease of mine on earth should run.
I've planned some work which still is far from done.
There's still a hill or two I wish to climb;
Come back, collector, at some other time."

"I've heard that story countless times before,"
Said the collector, standing at the door.
"You say you want more time! Well, Mr. Man,
Give me the date precisely, if you can.
Suppose I grant you five years more or ten,
Are you quite sure that you'll be ready then?

"When will your work be finished? Can you say
At fifty with a smile you'll go away?
At sixty shall I call? and will you then
Be glad to quit the fellowship of men?
Ah no, my friend, only the Master knows
The day and hour life's mortgage to foreclose!"

SUMMER

Bees are in the blossoms,
 Birds are on the wing,
Roses climb, and summertime
 Is kissing every thing.
Little pansy faces
 Wink and smile at me,
And far and near there's not a tear
 That human eye can see.

There's beauty in the garden,
 There's beauty in the sky,
The stately phlox and hollyhocks
 Have put their sorrows by.
The gentle breath of summer
 Has blown the cares away;
All nature sings, for morning brings
 Another lovely day.

Yet some are blind to beauty
 And some are deaf to song;
The troubled brow is heard to vow
 That all the world is wrong.
And some display their sorrow,
 And some bewail their woe
And some men sigh that love must die
 And summertime must go.

Yet some there are who blossom
  Like roses in the sun,
Who dare to climb in summertime
  When all their care is done.
They hide 'neath smiles of beauty
  The sorrows they have borne,
They seem content that God hath sent
  Another lovely morn.

THE CYNIC

In all this world of loveliness there lies
Some blemish to attract the cynic's eyes;
The rose of June is born of ache and hurt;
The cynic says: "Its roots are in the dirt."

A little child comes racing down the street;
The cynic says: " 'Twill grow to be a cheat."
Ground for a hospital a rich man buys;
The cynic jeers: "It pays to advertise."

Honor is doubted, mercy a mistake.
The marriage vow is only made to break;
The cheerful neighbor is a grinning fool,
And only idiots live by law and rule.

Yet youth goes blithely singing on its way,
And men and women brave the heat of day,
Finding life's beauty worth its cost in tears;
And joy exists, despite the cynic's sneers.

WHO GETS THE WATCH AND CHAIN

I've sat upon his left, and I
    Have sat upon his right,
I've heard him sob, I've heard him sigh,
    On many a banquet night.
Oh, we're a sentimental crew,
    The fact is very plain,
I'll prove it by the fellow who
    Receives the watch and chain.

He may appear a man severe,
    But let the speech begin,
And you can see the falling tear
    And mark the trembling chin.
He tries to speak, but seldom can,
    A fog obscures his brain,
I'm always sorry for the man
    Who gets the watch and chain.

I've sat where I could hear his heart
   In mortal anguish thump,
I've watched the grateful tear drops start,
   I've seen that awful lump
Come rising in his throat, and I
   Have wondered at his pain,
Why must the fellow always cry
   Who gets the watch and chain?

Man likes to pose as harsh and stern,
   But underneath his vest
Most of us some day come to learn
   He's easily distressed.
When he is honored by his clan
   His tears will fall like rain,
Grief always overcomes the man
   Who gets the watch and chain.

HER AWFUL BROTHER

Who teaches little Janet slang,
And trains those lips to say: "Gol Dang!"?
   Her awful brother!
Who whispers wise cracks in her ear
When none to stop his pranks is near?
   Her awful brother!

Who thinks up things for her to say
To shock her grandma day by day?
    Her awful brother!
Who laughs to hear her cry: "Oh, heck!"
Or "be your age!" And "wash your neck!"
    Her awful brother!

When friends have happened in for tea,
Who knows she'll mutter loud: "Oh gee!"
    Her awful brother!
Who likes to have his sister rough,
And fills her head with dreadful stuff?
    Her awful brother!

And yet, despite his love of mirth,
Who thinks that child the best on earth?
    That awful brother!
And who is it of whom she'll boast
And tell you that she loves the most?
    That awful brother!

THE FOOL

I'm the sort of a fool that will pull up a chair,
And then let a child come and rumple his hair,
And climb on his stomach and wiggle about,
Go through his pockets and empty them out,
And say when such mischievous rompings are done:
"Well, wasn't it fun?"

I'm the sort of a fool that will settle to read
A book, or a paper, a tract, or a screed,
And then let a blue-eyed and plump little maid,
Who of nobody living seems ever afraid,
Come right up and snatch what I'm reading away
Shouting: "Come, let us play!"

I'm the sort of a fool that will calmly sit by,
While a cute little finger is poked in his eye,
And a cute little foot kicks him square in the front
So hard that the neighbors are shocked at his grunt,
And then say with a grin when the fooling is done,
"Well, wasn't it fun!"

THE SINGING BIRD

Oh, singing bird! I wonder now and then,
Are you less troubled than world-weary men?
Do all your hopes come true, and is your nest
Always a sweet and happy place of rest?

I've seen you battle with your neighbors strong,
I fancy that at times you suffer wrong,
I know you must have fears, because the cat
Who seeks to take your life has taught me that.

Is yours an easy life? Have you no care?
That every morn I hear you singing there;
Do all your babies live? I hear no sigh.
In bird-life does no loved one ever die?

Man wails his lot and calls life harsh and rude,
Oh, happy bird! Do you not toil for food?
Have you no tasks which hold you fast by day?
Feel you no pains that you can seem so gay?

Ah yes, you share our cares, oh singing bird,
Yet from your throat there comes no scolding word!
In spite of all life's hurts, while you survive
You tell the world 'tis sweet to be alive!

THE HORN HONKER

The human family is queer.
  It does a lot of foolish things—
Too many to be printed here.
  We move when habit pulls the strings,
But there's one high above the rest
  Deserving of his fellow's scorn,
He is a nuisance and a pest—
  The driver with the honking horn.

When suddenly the traffic stops
  And twenty cars are in a line,
Held there by semaphores and cops
  And none may go without the sign,
Always some dull and empty mind
  Without a trace of reason born,
Who thinks he should not stay behind,
  Begins to toot upon his horn.

I wonder if he thinks that we
  Are staying there to please a whim,
Or lined up twenty deep to be
  A special barrier to him?
'Twould seem to any thinking man
  That were the roadway clear we'd go,
But he will start the caravan,
  He owns a horn which he can blow!

I've sat and wondered in a line,
    When traffic jams, as oft it will,
Just what this bird of queer design
    Imagines keeps us standing still.
Yet ever from the distant rear,
    At noon, or night, or early morn,
Somehow we always have to hear
    The senseless honker of the horn.

A FRIEND

A friend is one who stands to share
Your every touch of grief and care.
He comes by chance, but stays by choice;
Your praises he is quick to voice.

No grievous fault or passing whim
Can make an enemy of him.
And though your need be great or small,
His strength is yours throughout it all.

No matter where your path may turn
Your welfare is his chief concern.
No matter what your dream may be
He prays your triumph soon to see.

There is no wish your tongue can tell
But what it is your friend's as well.
The life of him who has a friend
Is double-guarded to the end.

THE YOUNG DOCTOR

They said he was a doctor six or seven months
 ago,
They gave him a diploma he could frame and
 proudly show,
And they said: "Go out and practice and just show
 'em what you know."

Now I've never been a doctor, but a lot of them
 I've met,
And that first year, so they tell me, is a year they
 won't forget—
With the practice slow in growing, and the mus-
 tache slower yet.

So I chuckled when I saw him, and his curious
 mustache,
And I chuckled when I heard him sob about his
 lack of cash,
And the scarcity of people with the measles or a
 rash.

"I've a very fine diploma," he explained, "upon a
 peg,
But if something doesn't happen I shall soon be
 forced to beg;
It's a lonely business waiting for some fool to break
 his leg."

The older doctors listened to his dismal tale of
     woe,
And a flood of reminiscence then it seemed began
     to flow—
They had all been youthful doctors in the distant
     long ago.

They had all sat down and waited through that
     terrifying year,
With their skill and knowledge ready for a promis-
     ing career;
They'd all grown those first mustaches so that
     older they'd appear.

I still see that youthful doctor with the sadness in
     his eye,
Sitting bravely in his office while the sick world
     travels by—
When that first poor patient finds him, Oh, I hope
     he doesn't die!

THE FLAG

"Why do we have a flag?" asked she,
 The greatest question box alive,
Astounding and perplexing me,
 Although her years are scarcely five.
"Why do we have a flag?" and I
Had never thought to wonder why.

"At first," said I, "when life began
 Then nothing very good was known.
The greatest was the strongest man.
 You've seen dogs fighting for a bone,
Well, human beings just that way
Fought for their food from day to day.

"Then men began to think and see
 A way that led to better things,
And little groups began to be,
 They formed in tribes and chose their kings,
And to distinguish clan from clan
The idea of a flag began.

"Then one flag meant we fight for land,
 Another for this king we'll die.
And soldiers battled, hand to hand,
 To keep their banner in the sky,
But in those ages long ago
There was so much they couldn't know.

"And many flags were trampled down,
    For men to learn are very slow;
That love and truth support a crown
    Was something that they didn't know.
And many bitter wars were fought
To pave the way for nobler thought.

"And now our flag is waving there
    To tell the world that you and I,
And all our neighbors everywhere
    Who fling Old Glory to the sky,
Are members of that mighty clan
Which seeks the betterment of man.

"Now when you see it in the skies,
    The red, the white and starry blue,
Remember as it proudly flies
    It's really representing you,
It's telling to the world afar
What kind of little girl you are."

THE YOUNGER GENERATION

This younger generation seems
  To mock at all our preaching;
To want to build its house of dreams
  Without our wiser teaching.

It looks at us with cool disdain
  And scorns the hints we're giving.
We've lived, of course, but all in vain;
  What do we know of living?

We are the kill-joys of the place
  Who cry: "Beware of strangers.
Sin lurks behind the smiling face.
  The streets are full of dangers."

So, poor old fogies that we are,
  We sit with fingers drumming,
The pale, despairing Pa and Ma
  Who dread what next is coming.

Ah, well! one time at counsel wise
  We sneered in youth's elation;
We scorned the old who would advise
  To seek our own salvation.

So why should we grow sorely vexed,
    Or trouble seek to borrow?
They'll be the kill-joys of the next
    Glad age which starts to-morrow.

The good advice they're heeding not
    They'll very soon be giving,
And hear *their* children wonder what
    They know of life and living.

PRAYER FOR A LITTLE GIRL

Dear Lord, our little baby bless
And fill her life with happiness.
Protect her through the coming years
And keep her lovely eyes from tears;
Keep her from pain and let her stay
As perfect as she is to-day.

Dear Lord, watch over her, lest she
Shall catch some ugly fault from me;
Guard her from selfishness and pride,
From anger at some whim denied.
And as the swift years come and go,
Grant that still lovelier she may grow.

Dear Lord, we ask, keep pure her mind,
Grant that no hasty thought may find
Lodgment therein, but from above
Send her the wisdom of Thy love.
May there be nothing base or vile
The joy of knowledge to defile.

Dear Lord, this for our babe we ask,
The strength and courage for her task,
Keep her from sin, and let her be
Always as radiant to see,
As beautiful and blithe and gay,
As perfect as she is to-day.

COUNTING THE BABIES

How many babies have you?
Well, really we've more than a few!
We've little Miss Laughter
And little Miss Pout,
And then there is little
Miss Scamperabout;
I never have counted them, good, bad and fair,
For the number is constantly changing I swear.

We've babies too many to tell,
We've little Miss Arrogant Belle,
We've little Miss Mischief
And little Miss Bold,

We've little Miss Whimper
And little Miss Scold.
And little Miss Hunger, who gets in the way,
Begging for cookies each hour of the day.

You'd not see them all in a week,
There's the bashful and little Miss Meek.
We've little Miss Blue Eyes
And little Miss Don't,
And that dreadful and
Troublesome little Miss Won't!
And the one that's as grasping as misers can be,
I refer to our little Miss Give It To Me!

I wish all their names that I knew,
There's little Miss Take Off Her Shoe.
There's little Miss Tippy-toe,
Little Miss Clutch,
Little Miss Sticky-thumbs,
Ruining much,
We've little Miss Drowsy, but need I keep on?
We've every known baby, and yet we've but one!

THE FUTURE

'Tis well enough to brag and boast,
But men who really do the most
   Sit very still.
They're very conscious all the time
To-morrow they will have to climb
   Another hill.
Nor all the little dreams come true
Make up for deeds they want to do.

Achievement is a pleasant thing,
But there's no end to conquering,
   And wise men see
That what is done, however fair,
Cannot in any way compare
   With what's to be.
And wise men's thoughts are ever turned
On secrets that are still unlearned.

I praise my skillful surgeon's hand.
"So much you've come to understand,"
   To him I say.
And then he smiles and whispers low;
"The things I really want to know
   Lie far away.
You think I've learned a lot, but oh,
There is so much I do not know!"

There is no conquest all complete;
No stopping place for human feet;
  No final goal.
Onward and upward men ascend
And none of us shall see the end
  Of glory's scroll.
But small and trivial is the past,
It is the future which is vast!

MEN OF SCIENCE

While ordinary mortals play
And laugh and dance the hours away,
The men of science, hid from sight,
Toil at their problems through the night
Within a laboratory room
Seeking to bring a thought to bloom.

We laugh and jest and eat and sleep,
The paths we tread are rutted deep,
The little tasks we're hired to face
Are known to all and commonplace,
But men of science fare alone
Into the future's great unknown.

From ceaseless toil at last there springs
One of the world's astounding things,
Proved beyond doubt and fit for fools
To place within their kits and tools,
And this becomes our common text:
"What will mankind discover next?"

We are the waiters of the world,
Debtors to every test tube curled;
The pale dependents on the few
Who bring to birth the glorious new.
Ours is to wonder while we live
What next the scientists will give.

A MOTHER FINDS REST

And now she dwells where neither doubt nor fear
    May find her breast;
No crying child may now disturb her here
    Or break her rest.

Ended the ache of living. Here she lies
    In wondrous peace.
God left a smile about her lovely eyes
    With her release.

How oft we fretted her or caused her pain,
  We cannot say.
Long hours she watched beside the window pane
  With us away.

Her sleep we broke with whimpering and sighs
  When we were ill.
Nor thought it much to rouse her with our cries,
  As children will.

But now we suffer so, and vainly call
  For her to come.
Her feet will never tread again the hall,
  Her lips are dumb.

Love had no more sweet service to provide,
  But this we know,
She'll watch for us upon the other side,
  Who tried her so.

IN TIME OF TRIAL

Oh, I have fared through laughter 'neath skies of
    summer blue!
And many an hour of mirth and joy I've danced
    and scampered through,
But, Lord, when joy was mine to know, I gave no
    thought to you.

I've had my days of pleasure and I've had my gold
    to spend,
But when my purse was plump and full I thought
    'twould never end,
And when I had no care to face I didn't need a
    friend.

I've whistled down the summer wind, I've sung a
    merry tune.
We never think of winter's snow when we are deep
    in June,
And no one dreams when pleasure calls that it will
    go so soon.

But, Lord, the skies are gray to-day and I am deep
    in care,
And I have need for help and strength my weight
    of grief to bear,
And so, like many an erring son, I turn to Thee in
    prayer.

WHO BUILDS A HOUSE

Who builds a house and plants a rose or two
   Gives to the world a symbol of his best;
Makes public pledge in all things to be true
   To meet with courage every bitter test.

His country can depend on him, for he
   Becomes a partner in her wealth and peace.
Who builds a house makes open guarantee
   That loyalty and faith shall never cease.

His friends must know him for an earnest man,
   His neighbors know he shares their hopes and
      fears.
Who builds a house does all that mortal can
   To show he will be steadfast through the years.

He is no nomad, moving with the night,
   No wanderer, drifting off from place to place.
Who builds a house has sworn to do the right,
   To be the strength and bulwark of his race.

God bless these houses where the brave men dwell,
   And keep them safe whatever storms descend;
Prosper their dreams and let their hopes go well.
   On them our glory and our peace depend.

BIRD NESTS

What a wonder world it is
   For a little girl of five
At the June time of the year,
   And so good to be alive,
With the meadows to explore,
   Seeking bird nests near and far,
And a dad of forty-four
   Who can show her where they are!

Every evening after tea
   We go wandering about
To the nests which we have found,
   Where the little birds are out.
And we tiptoe hand in hand
   To a certain lovely crest
Where delightedly we stand
   At a killdeer's curious nest.

And a meadow-lark we know
   With five babies of her own!
What a wonder world it is,
   And what miracles are shown!

She can scarcely stay for tea—
　　How she bolts her pudding through,
With so much she wants to see
　　And so much she wants to do!

So we hurry out of doors
　　And excitedly we race
To the mother meadow lark
　　And the killdeer's secret place.
And we talk of God Who made
　　All the birds and trees and flowers,
And we whisper, half afraid:
　　"What a wonder world is ours."

CANTERBURY BELLS

I stand and look about to-day
　　And something plainly tells
The gardens are expecting May
　　And Canterbury Bells.

I cannot hear the slightest sound,
　　But somehow I can feel
A certain bustling underground
　　That's very near and real.

Strange mysteries are going on
   Within the damp and gloom;
In worlds I cannot look upon
   The roses plan to bloom.

But I can only guess their plans
   And wait and watch them toil,
Convinced a greater work than man's
   Goes on below the soil.

The power of God I feel and see
   In every bud that swells,
In blossoms on the apple tree
   And Canterbury Bells.

TO A LITTLE GIRL

Little girl, just half-past three,
Take this little rhyme from me,
All the joy that gold can bring,
All the songs the birds can sing,
All this world can hold to give
Grown-up men the while they live,
Hath not half the charm of you
And the lovely things you do.

Little girl, just half-past three,
When God sent you down to me
Oft I wonder, did He know
Fortune's power would dwindle so?
Did He know that I should find
Such a curious change of mind,
And should some day come to see
Just how trivial pomp can be?

Little girl, just half-past three,
Lost are dreams that used to be.
Now the things I thought worth while
Could not buy your lovely smile,
And I would not give you up
For the golden plate and cup
And the crown a king may boast.
In my life you're uppermost.

Little girl, just half-past three,
This is what you mean to me,
More than all that money buys,
More than any selfish prize,
More than fortune, more than fame,
And I learned this when you came.
Other fathers know it, too.
Nothing matters more than you.

AN INTIMATE TALE

This is an intimate tale, a story of feminine wrath,
And a habit I've strangely acquired at the club when
I've finished my bath.
You must know how the folly began, for the cus-
tom is woman's, not man's,
But the golf club provides for our use a sweet-
scented powder in cans.
And I fancied the stuff must be cheap, for it's al-
ways supplied to us free,
So I stand when I come from my shower, shaking
violet talcum on me.

I flourish the can high and low, not a little I use,
but a lot.
I have said there's no charge for the stuff, so I fling
it around, and why not?
And some of it falls on the floor, but why should I
worry or care?
The stuff must be cheap, as I've said, or the club
wouldn't put it out there.
So I talcum myself front and back, and be waste-
fulness truly a sin,
Then I err at no cost to myself, and the stuff feels
so nice on the skin.

Now this habit so cheaply acquired has brought me
to grief and despair.

Last night as I came from my bath, the wife's box
of powder stood there,

And I just took it up and I shook, and shook as I
would at the club,

And some of it fell upon me, and some on the floor
and the tub.

But a few minutes later when she came into our
room, with a shriek

She told me what's what in a tongue which only a
woman can speak.

"Say, you!" she exclaimed in a voice denoting dis-
pleasure and fire,

"I'd a box full of powder to-day. Where is it? I
want to inquire."

"I've just used a little," I said, and a blush of shame
came to my cheek.

"A little!" she cried. "You have spilled far more
than I'd use in a week!

That stuff you have wasted on you, on your trousers,
your shoes and your socks,

Is the finest of powders from France, and it cost
me four dollars a box."

KIDNAPED BY A DREAM

My mind has run away with me,
  A kidnaped child am I;
A captive by a stretch of sea
  Beneath a sunny sky.
Here at my desk, a thought or two
Snatched me from all I ought to do.

And those who come in search of me
  Shall find me not to-day,
Unless they follow to the sea
  In much the self-same way;
My mind has rushed me out of town
Where ships are sailing up and down.

Oh, I was free an hour ago!
  But now with cords I'm tied
And none who pass me seem to know
  How oft for help I've cried;
My mind, against my will, I say
Has made me prisoner for the day.

To-night they'll find my task undone,
    Upon the page no word,
Perhaps there'll be a search begun
    To learn what has occurred,
But here will be no trace of me
Since I'm a captive, far at sea.

I thought myself secure, but no,
    This thing men call the mind
Caught hold of me and bade me go
    And leave all care behind.
Now when I tell this tale, I know
They'll smile and say it isn't so.

AT PINEHURST

Oh, to be at Pinehurst
  When spring is in the air!
And all the mutts and all the nuts
  Of golf are gathered there.
'Tis good to go to Boston,
  'Tis sweet to stop at Rye,
But I would go to Pinehurst
  Where all the golf balls fly.

The governors and statesmen
  Stand waiting on the tee,
The early ball has prior call
  Though kings behind may be.
And yonder in the bunker
  With curses in his throat
Is presidential timber
  And a diplomat of note.

The air is sweet at Pinehurst,
  The sky's a lovely blue,
But where you walk, the people talk
  Of swing and follow through.
The preacher is a golfer,
  God's blessing he invokes,
But the richest men at Pinehurst
  Are beggars wanting strokes.

And here I am at Pinehurst,
 For spring is in the air,
As Shakespeare said, the addled head
 Is little noticed there.
For though my game be faulty
 And erring is my pitch,
I'm giving strokes to beggars
 And succoring the rich.

A QUESTION OF SIGHT

Two travelers along a road,
Each weighted with the self-same load
 Of happiness and care,
Were chatting as they trudged ahead,
When suddenly one stopped and said:
"I see a farmhouse there!"

The other who was near-of-sight
Looked to the left and to the right,
 And said: "It cannot be.
There is no farmhouse where you say,
No roof or chimney down the way,
 No smoke that I can see."

"Look in the distance," cried his friend,
"There, where the road begins to bend,
    You'll catch a flash of light!"
"There is no farmhouse there," said he,
"At least, not one that I can see,
    Although you may be right."

"Well, never mind," his friend replied.
"Some day we'll reach it side by side,
    And you shall see it then."
"Perhaps," said he, "but as for me,
Nothing exists I cannot see."
    Thus quarreled two good men.

So with the great eternal life
Beyond this vale of mortal strife.
    Some glimpse a vision fair,
And some, not quite so keen of sight,
Peer vainly for the distant light
    And say it isn't there.

UNCHANGED

The "sweet sixteen" of old has disappeared;
  A wiser lovlier creature now we see.
To-day no man of thirty wears a beard,
  And grandma tries a youthful dame to be.
All ages play a swifter, faster game;
Thank heavens, childhood still remains the same!

Mothers no longer rock their babes to sleep;
  The flapper calls her father "dear, old bean!"
Age has no secrets now that it can keep;
  There's little left unmentioned or unseen.
The world has changed since Eve and Adam came;
Thank heavens, childhood still remains the same!

Women no longer boast their wealth of hair;
  The barber shops are double-sexed to-day.
Old men are dancing with a giddy air;
  The glories of the past have blown away.
What once was sport is now considered tame;
Thank heavens, childhood still remains the same!

Let fad and fashion sweep the wide world o'er;
  They cannot change the charm in little eyes.
The children still will romp about the floor
  And out of mud make chocolate cakes and pies.
Whatever else may come to praise or blame,
Thank heavens, childhood still remains the same!

THE COMMON DOG

One time there was a common dog who envied
      nobler breeds,
He noticed that their coats were smooth and free
      from burrs and seeds;
He saw them held in ladies' laps and following
      rich men's heels,
And learned they had good beds at night and most
      delicious meals.
And so he vowed unto himself that constantly he'd
      strive
To make himself as smooth and sleek as any dog
      alive.

And outwardly he turned the trick; he found a
      rich man's door
Who took him in and let him sleep upon his velvet
      floor.
He fed him well and brushed his coat; his tail to
      wag would start
To hear his master speak of him as a noble dog and
      smart;
But having come to luxury and fought that battle
      through
He thought he then could do the things that com-
      mon canines do.

And so he ran away at night and roamed the alleys, where

The dirty homeless dogs are found, and soiled his glossy hair.

And torn and tattered he'd return to everyone's disgust,

Until the rich man's wife declared; "Get rid of him you must!

This dog is just a common cur, as everyone must know,

He wasn't bred for luxury." And so they let him go.

Well, men at times work tricks like that, as everywhere appears;

To get to walk with millionaires they'll work and slave for years,

And when at last their fortune comes, they fling the barriers down

And chase the pleasures which belong to the commonest folks in town.

Then men and women everywhere disgusted turn and say:

"He wasn't bred for luxury or he wouldn't act that way."

NIGHT

When night comes down
To the busy town
  And the toilers stir no more,
Then who knows which
Is the poor or rich
  Of the day which went before?

When dreams sweep in
Through the traffic's din
  For the weary minds of men,
Though we all can say
Who is rich by day,
  Who can name us the rich man then?

It is only awake
The proud may take
  Much joy from the stuff they own,
For the night may keep
Her gifts of sleep
  For the humblest mortal known.

By day held fast
To creed and caste
  Men are sinner and saint and clown,
But who can tell
Where the glad hearts dwell
  When the dreams come drifting down?

LIFE ON THE EARTH

When they shall ask me over there
  What did you see, what did you do,
In what great splendors did you share?
  Tell us about the folks you knew,
I'll bet they'll smile to hear me say:
"I saw the tulips bloom in May."

Spring after spring I loved the breeze
  Which clover blossomed to perfume;
I watched the birds build nests in trees
  And saw the roses come to bloom.
For trout I used to wade the streams,
And had an endless stock of dreams.

The heart of me was often gay,
  Despite the cares I had to bear;
There never came a dreary day
  But what some loveliness was there;
And rich or poor or great or low,
The friends I made were good to know.

I had a little garlen there,
  A home where it was good to stay;
I'd food for all, and some to spare,
  And there were games I loved to play;
And though I sighed for pleasures lost,
Life on the earth was worth its cost.

TIME

Man impatient to possess
All he wants of happiness
   Works with feverish hands,
Striving for his whim to-day;
But Old Father Time says: "Nay!
   Toil and till your lands.
O'er that wall will ivy climb
Not to-morrow, but in time."

Man would have a maple tree
At a certain spot where he
   Wishes birds to nest.
"Now I'd have it!" is his cry;
"It may be that I shall die
   Ere it's at its best."
Father Time says: "Trees are slow,
Some take twenty years to grow."

Father Time is never swift
In the making of a gift;
   Slowly on he goes.
Man who wants life's beauty soon
Has to wait till middle-June
   For the budding rose.
Unto all who would be great
Father Time says: "Work and wait."

Oh be patient, eager man,
Life is purposed to a plan,
   Wisdom comes with years.
Time will teach you, as you grow,
Everything you want to know
   When the need appears.
Even mysteries sublime
You will understand in time.

THEN AND NOW

Oh, to be a boy again!
To live the old-time joy again,
To run with laughter everywhere
And seldom wince at pain;
To eat whatever food's in sight
With a perpetual appetite;
To grin at summer's burning sun
And laugh at autumn's rain.

Yet often though I wish again
To run and swim and fish again,
As did the care-free little boy
Who once I used to be,
I wouldn't backwards turn the page
And barter all the joys of age
To let some fairy steal my years
And make a boy of me.

Though much of joy was mine to know,
This older life is fine to know;
I walk with laughter still today
Despite my freight of care.
I'm sure I would not now enjoy
All things I cherished as a boy,
Nor wish to give my pleasures up
In boyhood's fun to share.

To life this is my attitude:
I have a sense of gratitude
For every joy which I have known;
A happy boy was I.
But it is fun a man to be,
And it is good to live and see
The richer beauty of the world
As time goes swinging by.

TWILIGHT

There come to me a few glad moments, when
   The busy day is ended, and I stray
Into the garden, shut away from men
   And all their tasks and all the sports they play.

The birds are homing for the coming night,
   The air is still and peaceful and serene,
But there's a beauty in the fading light
   Which at the noon of day is seldom seen.

Pansies and poppies, peonies and phlox,
   All with a long day's toil complete to view!
Trees which have stood perennial storms and shocks,
   Old as the world, yet always young and new.

I walk among them where the shadows fall,
   And seem to feel in touch with things divine;
Who knows, but I am brother to them all,
   Brother to bluebell, rose and columbine?

THEORY AND PRACTICE

Twixt theory and practice lies
  A chasm wide and deep.
With theory the brilliant wise
  A bivouac nightly keep,
While heavy hearts and weary eyes
  Turn from their toil to sleep.

Life is not what it ought to be,
  The theorists declare;
But this the eyes of all can see
  For wrong is everywhere:
Rain falls the very day that we
  Have prayed for weather fair.

And there are hurts which seem unjust
  And dreams which go astray;
In spite of all our care we must
  Face many a bitter day:
Sometimes the one we've grown to trust
  Flings all our faith away.

But he is happiest here who moves
  Serenely towards his goal,
Who does not set his life in grooves
  But sees it as a whole,
And meeting joy or sorrow, proves
  The valor of his soul.

TO THE JUNE BRIDE

The groom is at the altar, and the organ's playing
low,
Young and old, your friends are waiting, they are
sitting row by row.
Now your girlhood's all behind you, in a few brief
minutes more
You'll be wife to him who's waiting, through the
years that lie before.

Oh, I say it not to daunt you, but to strengthen you
for fate,
In the distance for your coming many heavy trials
wait.
Whoso enters into marriage takes a very solemn
vow
To be faithful to the other when the days are not
as now.

Arm in arm you'll walk together through the lane of
many years,
Side by side you'll reap life's pleasures, side by side
you'll shed your tears;

'Tis a long road you'll be faring, for I've journeyed
    half the way,
But if love and faith sustain you you will triumph,
    come what may.

There's the happy time of marriage, but to every
    man and wife
Also come the hurts and sorrows and the bitterness
    of life;
For by these your faith is tested, 'tis by these your
    love shall grow,
And my prayer is love shall guide you wheresoever
    you shall go.

THE HOME

Write it down that here I labored,
Here I sang and laughed and neighbored;
Here's the sum of all my story,
Here's my fortune and my glory;
These four walls and friendly door
Mark the goal I struggled for.
Never mind its present worth,
Here's one hundred feet of earth
Where the passer-by can see
Every dream which came to me.

Write it down: my life uncloses
Here among these budding roses;
In this patch of lawn I've tended,
Here is all I've counted splendid;
Here's the goal that's held me true
To the tasks I've had to do.
Here for all the world to scan
Is my secret thought and plan;
Through the long years gone before,
This is what I struggled for.

Write it down, when I have perished:
Here is everything I've cherished;
That these walls should glow with beauty
Spurred my lagging soul to duty;
That there should be gladness here

Kept me toiling, year by year.
Here in phlox and marigold
Is my every purpose told;
Every thought and every act
Were to keep this home intact.

THE WILD FLOWERS

Men cover the earth with brick and stone
   But the violets steal away
To the shady places but little known
To be found by some one who walks alone
   In the calm of a summer day.

And the ferns move out to some distant spot
   Where the earth is cool and sweet;
With trees and song birds they cast their lot,
Let men build cities, they like them not,
   Nor the ceaseless tramp of feet.

The wild flowers sneer at man's buildings great
   And flee from the city's hum;
Away from turmoil and pride and hate
They live and bud and blossom, and wait
   For the few friends who may come.

AT THE JOURNEY'S END

Come, death, be merciful and end his pain!
Life has deserted him and hope is vain.
You were his foe, but at the journey's end
Now he would welcome you and call you friend.

The life he loved is over. All is done!
He is too tired to greet the morning sun,
He is too tired for laughter or for care,
Strike the last blow and let him slumber there.

No bright to-morrow here for him can dawn,
The last sweet joys of earth for him are gone,
Anguish and pain are all life has to give,
He longs for sleep, but sleep life cannot give.

Come, death, be friendly—end his bitter pain,
Seal those brave lips which shall not smile again.
We who must stay shall weep that he must go;
Peace comes with death—and it were better so.

MEMORIAL DAY

Now the living come to spread
Flowers above their hero dead;
Now above each silent grave
Flies the flag they died to save.

Drums are tapped and bugles blown,
Voices in a muffled tone
Speak of them, as proof that we
Hold them all in memory.

But I wonder, do they hear?
Are their spirits hovering near?
Can they with a clearer sight
See and read our hearts aright?

These, our little gifts of flowers,
Wither in a few brief hours:
With the midnight shall we say
Done is our Memorial day?

Can we truly tell that we
Hold them long in memory,
Save the faith in us survives
Which to keep they gave their lives?

God, this tribute let us give,
Bravely for their cause we live;
All the dreams for which they died
Still within our breasts abide.

I MAKE AN EXPERIMENT

The boy that hangs about my frame
Has left the old man stiff and lame;
The youngster that delights to stay
Within this aging house of clay
As lively as he used to be
Has made a sorry wreck of me.

I wince with every muscle twinge,
I creak at every ancient hinge;
The sprightly step I had is gone,
Today I merely totter on
And all because that youthful soul
Insisted that I still could bowl.

'Tis more than twenty years ago
Since last I stooped a ball to throw,
But still I'd not forgotten how,
And though there's silver at my brow
That boy, who mocks at fading hair,
Just itched once more to strike and spare.

And so, despite my aging frame,
I tried once more that famous game;
That ball which once with ease I threw
Now seemed to weigh a ton or two,
And strangely, too, I ought to say,
Those ten pins seemed a mile away.

This morning, tired and muscle sore,
A sad old man I walk the floor;
And though my spirit still is fresh
I am a lump of worn out flesh.
Hearts may stay young, as we are told,
But this I know—man's joints grow old.

A MODERN CLOTHESLINE

Time was that on Mondays the washing was done
And the clothes hung to dry in the warmth of the
      sun,
And they flapped in the breeze for the whole world
      to see,
But the sight was as drab and as plain as could be;
For the garments of old were of white or of gray
And they looked all alike in that old-fashioned day.

On Mondays the family washing's still done
And hung out to dry in the warmth of the sun,
And it flaps in the breezes, but strange to behold!
There's a blend now of orchid and scarlet and gold;
The drabness has vanished. The passer-by views
A radiant clothesline of marvelous hues.

I passed by a clothesline and chuckled in mirth,
It seemed that a rainbow had fallen to earth,
With its lavender tints blended there with the pink
And the fluffies of yellow, called step-ins, I think;
And I said as I looked at those purples and tans,
"The only plain things on that line are a man's!"

SUCCESS

Success is doing something well,
  It's winning faith and trust,
Despite what theorists may tell
  It's doing what you must;
It's giving all the best of you
To every task you have to do.

Success is not the gift of luck
  When rightly understood,
It's keeping on with grit and pluck
  To make your service good;
It's keeping honest, when you meet
An easy chance to play the cheat.

Success is in the will to be
  On friendly terms with men,
It's in little things they'll see
  When next you meet again;
For nothing ever lives so long
Or works such havoc as a wrong.

Who gives his best to every task,
  Who keeps the faith with all,
For friends will never have to ask
  Or for assistance call:
But who with any trust does less
Will never be a real success.

THE CITY HOME

Although the motors rush along
   And wild flowers grow no more,
And fled are all the birds of song
   To nest beyond the roar,
Although the trees are coming down
   To make more room for men,
'Tis home within the busy town
   To which I turn again.

'Tis not a winding lane I fare
   But one that's straight and wide,
The pavements now are cold and bare,
   Long since the flowers have died:
But still I keep a patch of grass,
   And save a rose or two
For all the busy men who pass
   In summertime to view.

The city home is on a street
   Where once the wild flowers grew,
And once the song birds used to meet
   On meadows wet with dew:
Now wall by wall the houses stand,
   And all the trees have gone,
And concrete covers far the land
   The cattle grazed upon.

For commerce drives the birds away
    With all its noisy roar,
And speeds its motors day by day
    Where wild flowers grew before;
And progress builds the busy town
    By piling bricks in air,
But still it's home when night comes down,
    And all life's joys are there.

A BOMBING SQUAD FLIES OVER

Overhead the airplanes fly,
    Fifteen birds in echelon,
Fifteen monarchs of the sky
    And a boy in every one.

Overhead the motors roar,
    From their nooks the pigeons fly,
Refugees that race before
    These invaders of the sky.

Startled pigeons, well I know
    Why you wildly dart and wheel;
Here's a strange and ugly foe
    Come your lovely sky to steal.

Now they're swooping down again,
    Fifteen boys in perfect line;
Watching through my window pane,
    Terror, such as yours, is mine.

I am fearful of this thing
    Rushing, roaring through the sky,
Fifteen young hearts, wing to wing!
    Of an older age am I.

Youth may laugh and mock at me,
    But my old heart beats with fear;
This is danger that I see,
    Danger very real and near.

THE WORST OF PESTS

I do not mind the driver who would faster go than I;
I will quickly, when he signals, turn aside to let
    him by:
For the driver of the taxi I am glad to turn aside,
He is busy earning money, not just out to take a
    ride:
But the driver I can't stand for, be his car of steel
    or tin,
Is that chap who blocks the traffic by his selfish
    edging in.

There's the boy who races signals—let him rush
    along his way—
For the officer will get him in the end and he will
    pay;
I can chuckle at the driver, though he rouses others'
    scorn,
Who displays his restless spirit by the honking of
    the horn:
But the one who most disturbs me, in the city's rush
    and din,
Is the chap who crowds his fellows and insists on
    edging in.

The stop sign never stops him—he keeps crawling
    on his way,
And he shows no thought for others or the law he
    should obey:
Though a dozen cars are coming, he won't leave
    their pathway clear,
They must stop to let him over or profanity they'll
    hear:
And I always get a chuckle and I always get a grin
When somebody strips a fender from the chap who
    edges in.

THE CHILDREN KNOW

Old folks see the tulips red
Growing in my garden bed;
Childhood with a clearer sight
Peeps into the blossoms bright,
And upon a silver chair
Sees a fairy sitting there.

Old folks walk my garden round
With an air that's most profound,
Seeing here and there a weed,
Noting blossoms gone to seed;
Little Janet, though, can tell
Visitors where goblins dwell.

Age which knows so much can see
All the dead limbs on the tree,
Every blemish round the place;
Janet, with a happier face,
Has a thousand charms to show,
Charms which only children know.

INDEX OF FIRST LINES

Page

A friend is one who stands to share.....134
All-day suckers and lollypops.....107
Although the motors rush along.....181
And now she dwells where neither doubt nor fear.....145
An oak tree died the other day.....32
A public speaker's lot is not an easy one to bear..113
A thousand men filed in by day.....77
Aunt Jane was one of the worrying kind.....92

Bees are in the blossoms.....126
Beneath the stars at night when all was clear.....112

Come, death, be merciful and end his pain!.....175

Dead they left Him in the tomb.....71
Dear Lord, for food and drink and peace.....96
Dear Lord, our little baby bless.....140
Death, the collector, came to him and said.....125
Dreams are for a summer's day!.....58

Ed and John were little boys in the long ago.....43

Figure it out for yourself, my lad.....91
For fish and birds I make this plea.....74
From birth to death the pathway leads.....26

Give us more lovers of beauty.....121
God builds no churches!.....82
God grant me this: the right to come at night.....53
Gold is found in the hills.....44
Grant me, O Lord, this day to see.....31

His life was gentle, and his mind.....93
How many babies have you?.....141
How strange is age, that season of decay.....22

Index of First Lines

	Page
I can be happy in a boat	86
I do not mind the driver who would faster go than I	183
If I knew a better land on this glorious world of ours	33
If I were asked one thing to name	47
If to be clever means that I must sneer	95
If wealth were all a man required	54
If youth had been willing to listen	106
If you walk as a friend you will find a friend	27
I had a full day in my purse	79
I had an old, tired car	64
I have a life I can't escape	75
I like to see a lovely lawn	69
"I'm a golfer, St. Peter!"	65
I'm just an old fool	25
"I'm not a philosopher, bearded and gray"	63
I'm the sensitive soul that is known as the dub!	116
I'm the sort of a fool that will pull up a chair	131
In all this world of loveliness there lies	127
I never see a gallant ship go steaming out to sea	103
Into my room a stranger came	87
"I played so badly," said the organist	124
I sometimes get weary of people	18
I stand and look about to-day	150
It doesn't matter much be its buildings great or small	111
It's all very well to have courage and skill	105
It's good to do the hard job	101
I've never worn a high silk hat	118
I've sat upon his left, and I	128
Life is queer and people move	70
Little girl, just half-past three	151
Looking back, it seems to me	50
Man impatient to possess	165
Men cover the earth with brick and stone	174

Index of First Lines

Page

Money and fame and health alone 21
Much I've done and much I've seen 15
My grandpa once was very sick 17
My mind has run away with me 155
My son, when plans have gone astray 115

Now the living come to spread 176

Oh, bride and groom, the day is fair 85
"Oh, if only I had known!" 23
Oh, I have fared through laughter 147
Oh, let me have my work to do 102
Oh, once I sent a ship to sea 109
Oh, singing bird! I wonder now and then 132
Oh, the days I've wasted 78
Oh, to be a boy again! 167
Oh, to be at Pinehurst 157
Oh, whether it's business or whether it's sport 108
Old folks see the tulips red 185
Once there was a little girl who wouldn't go to
     bed 59
One broken dream is not the end of dreaming 97
One time I told a giant tale before she went to
     bed 99
One time there was a common dog 161
Overhead the airplanes fly 182

Shame seldom gets the man who sees 119
Some look at care as if it should not be 123
Some say that chance or guess or hazard makes .. 117
Sometimes I get to thinkin' o' the days o' youth .. 19
Success is doing something well 180

The boy that hangs about my frame 177
The dentist tinkered day by day 83
The groom is at the altar 171
The human family is queer 133
The joy of getting home again 57
The keys to the car! 39

Page

The mind is that mysterious thing.................... 67
The old-time barber used to be a genial sort of
    cuss 41
There are two worlds wherein to dwell................ 81
There come to me a few glad moments................169
There is many a battle that's yet to be won........ 51
There was action in the old days........................ 90
There was a man I once knew well...................... 73
The salesman saw his shabby clothes.................. 36
The "sweet sixteen" of old has disappeared.....,...160
The weakest excuses of all the lot...................... 98
The woods and fields and trees are ours.............122
They said he was a doctor...................................135
They say life's simple—but I don't know............ 55
This is an intimate tale......................................153
This is what a man likes........................... •.... 35
This younger generation seems...........................139
Time was that on Mondays the washing was
    done 179
'Tis well enough to brag and boast....................143
To-day as I was starting out.............................. 49
Twixt theory and practice lies............................170
Two travelers along a road.................................158

Up and down the lanes of love............................ 45

Well, you see, I met your mother at a wedding.... 29
What a wonder world it is...................................149
"What this house is going to be"........................ 61
When first I met your father.............................. 27
When night comes down.....................................163
When sages old on life reflect............................104
When the bees are in the clover.......................... 89
When they shall ask me over there......................164
While ordinary mortals play..............................144
Who builds a house or plants a rose or two........148
Who teaches little Janet slang............................129
"Why do we have a flag?" asked she...................137
Write it down that here I labored.......................173